Introduction
vol. 1 –
yellow
highlighting

3 volume
set

VOLUME ONE

Wilhelm Meister's Years of Apprenticeship

By the same author

Kindred by Choice

The Sufferings of Young Werther

VOLUME ONE

WILHELM MEISTER'S YEARS OF APPRENTICESHIP

Wilhelm Meisters Lehrjahre

by

Johann Wolfgang von Goethe

Translated by
H. M. Waidson

JOHN CALDER
LONDON

This translation from the German, first published in 1977 by John Calder (Publishers) Ltd., 18 Brewer Street, London W1R 4AS

ISBN 0 7145 3675 X Cased

Typeset by the Blackburn Times Press, Northgate, Blackburn Lancashire BB2 1AB in 10pt Plantin. Printed by M. & A. Thomson Litho, East Kilbride. Bound by Hunter and Foulis Ltd., Edinburgh.

CONTENTS

INTRODUCTION

It is indicative of Goethe's many-sided literary achievements that he had unique, major contributions to make to lyrical poetry, drama and prose writing. The novel *Wilhelm Meister,* it has long been generally accepted, occupies a central, pivotal position in German literature, and it has exerted a great influence from the time of the first publication of the *Years of Apprenticeship* onwards, firstly upon Romantic writers, subsequently upon realists of the nineteenth century, and later upon twentieth-century authors including, for instance, such as Thomas Mann and Hesse. As a major novel *Wilhelm Meister* has much substantial and varied material to offer readers, both in the *Years of Apprenticeship* and in the later sequel, the *Years of Travel.* The first characteristic of the *Years of Apprenticeship* to be noticed is its pursuit of the theme of an individual's personal development in relation to a broad spectrum of society, to a series of clearly and realistically portrayed milieux, and to the age in which he lives. The point of view that is predominantly shown is that of the central figure as he passes through years of early manhood, and as on occasions he evokes recollections of his childhood. The term 'Bildungsroman', coined with *Wilhelm Meister* and novels like it in mind, includes the idea of the formation of the individual personality, both through inner effort and outward influence, and that of the unfolding of natural potentialities. Progress is from error and confusion to truth and clarity, and as the novel proceeds it makes or implies judgments on what may be right or wrong from the point of view of the hero's development in life. Such a novel is ultimately optimistic; the central figure will keep on striving, and others will help him, in a variety of ways, in his quest for fulfilment. Constructive lessons will be taught, in the manner of the Age of Enlightenment, as this was interpreted by Goethe and his intellectual associates in the late eighteenth century. The outcome is utopian, as there is the hope that the ideal of a higher form of humanity can be realized in earthly society.

None the less it is the inner, emotional life of Wilhelm that is presented to us in the first place, and it is not long before it becomes evident how sensitive and fragile it is, and how easily it can be hurt. His early happiness is followed by a protracted depression after the collapse of his relationship with Mariane; the recovery is slow and there are vacillations and wrong turnings before something akin to what we are intended to accept as the right track is taken. Whereas Goethe's first novel, *The Sufferings of Young Werther,* published twenty years prior to the *Years of Apprenticeship,* had described a highly-strung inner life that terminated in suicide, Wilhelm's emotional self is allowed less overwhelming dominance and in due course finds its own adjustments to the outer world. But elements of fateful, uncanny mystery remain throughout the *Years of Apprenticeship,* particularly in the two vulnerable figures whom Wilhelm protects—the girl Mignon, on the verge of adolescence, and the Harpist, the older musician bowed down by a sense of doom.

The *Years of Apprenticeship* is divided into two major sections; the first five of the eight books focus attention on Wilhelm's early life, and offer us what seems to be a novel mainly about the theatre, while 'The Confessions of a Beautiful Soul' form an interlude before the hero, in books seven and eight, is finally removed from the theatre environment and accepts the guidance of the Society of the Tower and becomes part of a family that has the will and the means to foster intellectual and cultural ideals and ultimately to point the way to a new society.

Wilhelm, who comes from a prosperous urban mercantile family, acquires an enthusiasm for the theatre at an early age. His fascination with theatre and drama is not only on an individualistic, aesthetic basis, but is the expression of a concern for society, particularly for German society, at this time. For the younger generation of the German middle classes in the mid-eighteenth century the stage-play could represent a possible means to group, indeed national fulfilment. In the earlier books of the novel Wilhelm is full of hopes for the German theatre of the near future and the leading part he would like to play in its development What is envisaged in a national theatre is an institution that should draw together the differing, separate social groups; the theatres based on princely courts were evidently exclusive, and the travelling players provided humbler entertainment. A national theatre, supported by public funds, should be non-commercial and could be proud of a didactic, moral tendency. The experiment sponsored by business-men in Hamburg to which Lessing was invited as resident dramatic critic and adviser was a venture that did not survive for long, any more than Wilhelm's association with Serlo. On the day-to-day level too Wilhelm soon finds that a number of the actors he is associating with have little or no interest in the literary qualities of plays, are haphazard in their approach to traditions, are untidy, careless, and generally lacking in stability and purpose. Wilhelm brings the criteria of his own middleclass family background to the assessment of the stage; but in spite of the criticism, the fascination remains for a long time. Both actors and aristocracy are presented here as having a strong sense of sociability together with a proclivity for intrigue, which the novelist depicts with not a little irony.

If Wilhelm hopes to please the Prince (in Book Three) by commending his fondness for seventeenth century French classicism, in particular for Racine, he is immediately afterwards recommended by Jarno to read Shakespeare. French classicist style is associated with court circles and public occasions, but the impact of Shakespeare on Wilhelm now is emotional, impassioned and inward, deriving from solitary reading. The advocacy of French plays for the German stage, especially by Gottsched in the seventeen-thirties and seventeen-forties was challenged by Lessing in his seventeenth 'Letter on Literature' (1759) where Shakespeare is offered as an alternative model. Goethe's own discovery of Shakespeare, when under the temporary tutelage of Herder in Strassburg, soon called forth the lively adventure drama *Götz von Berlichingen;* the *Sturm und Drang* mood of the earlier seventeen-seventies included Rousseau inspired nature-feeling and the revival of the folksong as well as the cult of Shakespeare.

The first certain reference to *Wilhelm Meister* is a diary entry of February 1777. Goethe's major work on that earlier part of the novel centring upon Wilhelm's involvement with the theatre took place after 1775, when the author established his independence of the atmosphere of his youth and his parental home at Frankfurt by his move to Weimar, and up to 1786, when the journey to Italy brought another break in his life, and the opportunity to look with some perspective at the eleven years during which he had been first adjusting to the Weimar court atmosphere. In his early Weimar years Goethe was himself, like Wilhelm at the Count's country house, writing for the court stage, acting in an amateur capacity (in the prose version of *Iphigenie auf Tauris* in 1779, where he made it clear that a classicist style was now in fact very sympathetic to him) and busying himself with all sorts of practical details concerning productions there. *Wilhelm Meisters theatralische Sendung (Wilhelm Meister's Theatrical Mission)* is the title of that manuscript of Goethe's, not discovered and made generally available until 1910, which consists of an extensive fragment; six books of the twelve originally planned were written. This earlier version is different in many ways from the first four books of the *Years of Apprenticeship* into which the author compressed and rewrote the material after his Italian journey. However, it seems likely that even in the *Theatrical Mission* the author was already distancing himself to some degree from his hero's enthusiasms, and that it was by no means certain that Wilhelm was to have his aspirations for the theatre in Germany successfully and permanently realized.

The final phase of work on the *Years of Apprenticeship*, after the return from Italy, makes it fully clear that the author no longer attached a great deal of positive social merit to his hero's preoccupation with the theatre. It is true, the stage may be seen as offering a life embodying vitality and some fulfilment for Wilhelm in contrast to the dessicating effects which the business-man's life has on Werner; but Wilhelm's appearance as Hamlet in Book Five marks the culmination and close of his theatre career. Henceforth he has to go in another direction. It is interesting to note that at that time when the novelist's didactic purpose was leading Wilhelm away from the theatre, Goethe himself took on a new commitment in this very field; he became artistic director of the professional court theatre at Weimar in 1791, and continued in that office until 1817. In 1791 he directed a production of Shakespeare's *King John*, and early the next year *Hamlet* was produced. Even if Goethe's later attitude to Shakespeare is markedly guarded, his broad and sustained presentation of Wilhelm's concern about Shakespeare is historically a very considerable contribution to the German reception of that dramatist.

Book Four introduces Wilhelm to the personality and theatre of Serlo, envisaged as the leading German theatrical manager and producer of his age. For a time Wilhelm believes that association with Serlo's theatre in the large, bustling northern city will bring him the vocational satisfaction he longs for. In the private sphere the protective element in Wilhelm's nature finds expression in his friendship with Serlo's sister Aurelia in the period of her illness and intense distress shortly before her death. On receiving the news of his father's death (at the opening of Book Five) Wilhelm feels free from the duty of paying consideration to the mercantile form of life that he finds irksome, and he goes ahead with his plans to take the title-role in *Hamlet*. The uncertainty and hesitancy of his nature are again emphasized; he is reluctant to make conscious decisions, preferring to let himself be carried along by impulse. A number of the turning-points in his life are being guided by the Society of the Tower, which centres upon the family group that acts as a form of secular providence to him.

The 'Confessions of a Beautiful Soul' (Book Six) are presented as a manuscript by a concerned doctor to Aurelia so that she may be comforted by its message as she lies fatally ill. Goethe wrote this account in part as a memorial to Susanna von Klettenberg, a friend of his mother's and a member of the pietistic religious circle with which he had been in sympathy as a young man after leaving Leipzig and before going to Strassburg as a student. The fictitious autobiography has an apparently quiet and simple succession of events, and is thus a respite from much in the account of Wilhelm's adventures hitherto in the bustle of the theatre world and on the fringe of intrigue in aristocratic circles. A lady who has remained single looks back upon her life and interprets it from the viewpoint of her religious inwardness. Wilhelm is to have sympathetic understanding of this approach, but will himself go on (in Books Seven and Eight) to the absorption of a secular humane idealism, where artistic and cultural values and a will to practical service of one's fellow-men are integral.

Although Wilhelm puts the theatre behind him, it is only with some reluctance that he comes to accept the tutelage of the Society of the Tower. His immediate reason for making the contact is to confront Lothario with his guilt at having deserted Aurelia, but now that the time is ripe the family envelops him with hospitality and care. The death of the Uncle, the presiding father-figure of the Society of the Tower, at the end of Book Seven coincides with the formal declaration to Wilhelm that his years of apprenticeship are over and that a further responsibility now awaits him, the care for the boy Felix, his and Mariane's son. This might seem to be a reasonable point at which to terminate the *Years of Apprenticeship*, but the author adds in Book Eight a further series of episodes which are to bring various aspects of the plot to a conclusion. Wilhelm, while divided in his mind between the attractions of Theresa and Natalie, has his last outburst of resentment against the family's guidance; but this is overcome, and the marriage with Natalie signals acceptance of membership of this group. The deaths of Mignon and the Harpist may be taken as indicating the removal of irrational, daemonic influences in Wilhelm's life, while at the same time recalling that if Wilhelm is to be guided to the domain of light, others may suffer and come to an end that is premature or dark.

Thus the *Years of Apprenticeship* is rounded off and might well have been seen in 1796 as a fully self-contained and complete work; indeed, this was the form in which the novel exercised its wide influence on subsequent German writing. However, Goethe was already talking about writing a sequel in 1796, and some motifs find their place at the close of the *Years of Apprenticeship*. Wilhelm and his son Felix are undertaking an extensive journey as the *Years of Travel* open; to some degree this is part of a continuing general education, but it can also be seen as a study in social conditions to assist the Society of the Tower which owns land in America and is planning to establish a new community there. Just as Jarno in the *Years of Apprenticeship* had given Wilhelm's thought about the theatre an important new direction by introducing him to Shakespeare's work, so now he persuades Wilhelm that the ideal of general self-development is inadequate and that the new age can best be served by a renunciation of the aspiration to the rounded personality; specialization is seen as a form of ascetic achievement. Wilhelm now makes the particular decision to become a medical doctor, so that he can serve his fellows in this direct and socially constructive manner. There is a caesura of some years in the novel while he undergoes medical training, during which the Society's plans for emigration have ripened further. The feeling emerges that Europe is approaching a time of crisis in consequence of its increasing population and of the development of mass, industrial society. Lothario's American land will allow a new community to be established, one that is modelled in part on William Penn's settlement in Pennsylvania and anticipated within the novel itself in the organization of the boarding school which Felix attends for a while. The concluding episode of the *Years of Travel* shows Wilhelm able to make use of his newly acquired practical skill by aiding his son when the latter is in distress. The theme of renunciation indicated in the sub-title of the *Years of Travel* ('or those who renounce') is further illustrated in a series of inset-stories where love-interest predominates; *Kindred by Choice* was first conceived by Goethe as a short tale in this context, but having taken hold of its author's mind with particular tenacity it developed into the novel that was published in 1809.

The *Years of Travel,* whose definitive version appeared in 1829, reflects some of Goethe's ideas on society in a world that was adjusting itself to the new shape of Europe that emerged after 1815; the *Years of Apprenticeship* describe a world that did not anticipate the French Revolution of 1789 and what was to follow. The whole work offers a rich, broad panorama as well as frequent penetration in depth into poignant personal problems. It is a major novel in European literature.

Select Bibliography

Here are a few references for further reading; in most cases these works include bibliographical information:

GOETHE, 'Weimarer' or 'Sophienausgabe', 143 vols., 1887-1920 (*Wilhelm Meisters Lehrjahre* in vols. 21-23); 'Hamburger Ausgabe', 21 vols., 1948-69 (*Lehrjahre* in vol. 7); 'Gedenkausgabe', 27 vols., 1948-71 (*Lehrjahre* in vol. 7). [Erich Trunz's notes in vol. 7 of the 'Hamburger Ausgabe' have been gratefully used; the footnotes in the text that follows derive mainly from this source.]

BLACKALL, E. A., *Goethe and the Novel* (1976)

BRUFORD, W. H., *Theatre, drama and audience in Goethe's Germany* (1950)

BRUFORD, W. H., *Culture and society in Classical Weimar, 1775-1805* (1962)

FAIRLEY, B., *A study of Goethe* (1947)

GRAY, R.; *Goethe: A critical introduction* (1967)

KORFF, H. A. *Geist der Goethezeit* (1923-41)

MÜLLER, G., *Kleine Goethe-Bibliographie* (1947)

PASCAL, R., *The German novel* (1956)

REISS, H., *Goethe's novels* (1969)

STAIGER, E., *Goethe* (1952-59)

VIETOR, K., *Goethe* (1948)

Principal Dates of Goethe's Life

1749	Born at Frankfurt am Main
1765	Studied at Leipzig
1770-71	Studied law at Strassburg
1772	Spent some months in Wetzlar at the supreme court of the Empire
1773	*Götz von Berlichingen* (prose drama)
1774	*Clavigo* (prose drama)
1774	*Die Leiden des jungen Werthers* (novel)
1775	Becomes companion to the young Duke Karl August at Weimar and subsequently becomes much involved in administrative work there.
1786-88	Journey to Italy
1787	*Iphigenie auf Tauris* (verse drama)
1788	*Egmont* (prose drama)
1788	After returning to Weimar from Italy, beginning of relationship with Christiane Vulpius.
1789	*Torquato Tasso* (verse drama) Birth of August, son of Goethe and Christiane.
1790	*Faust. Ein Fragment* (verse drama)
1791	Becomes artistic director of the Weimar court theatre, remaining in this office until 1817.
1792-93	Accompanies the Duke Karl August on campaign against France.
1795	*Unterhaltungen deutscher Ausgewanderten* (prose fiction)
1795	*Römische Elegien* (cycle of poems)
1795-96	*Wilhelm Meisters Lehrjahre* (novel)
1797	*Hermann und Dorothea* (verse epic)
1803	*Die natürliche Tochter* (verse drama)
1806	Marriage to Christiane
1808	*Faust. Erster Teil* (verse drama)
1809	*Die Wahlverwandtschaften* (novel)
1809	*Pandora* (masque in verse)
1811-33	*Dichtung und Wahrheit* (autobiography)
1816	Death of Christiane
1816-17	*Italienische Reise* (autobiography)
1819	*West-östlicher Divan* (cycle of poems)
1828	*Novelle* (prose fiction)
1829	*Wilhelm Meisters Wanderjahre* (final version of the second part of the novel)

PRINCIPAL DATES OF GOETHE'S LIFE

1832	Death of Goethe
1833	*Faust. Der Tragödie zweiter Teil* (verse drama)

BOOK ONE

Chapter One

The performance went on a very long time. Old Barbara stepped to the window several times, listening for the rattle of carriages. She was waiting for her pretty mistress Mariane with greater impatience than usual, even though she had only a modest supper to put before her; Mariane was delighting the audience that evening in the dramatic epilogue, in the guise of a young officer; on this occasion she was to be surprised by a package which Norberg, a young and wealthy merchant, had sent in order to show that even at a distance he thought of his beloved.

As old servant, confidante, adviser, agent and housekeeper Barbara had the right to open the seals, and on this evening too she found it all the more difficult to restrain her curiosity as the attentions of the generous lover meant more to her than to Mariane herself. She was overjoyed to find that the package contained a fine piece of muslin and the latest in ribbons for Mariane, while for herself were a piece of cotton, neckerchiefs and a rouleau of money. With what affection and gratitude did she remember the absent Norberg! How enthusiastically did she resolve to mention him most favourably in Mariane's presence, to remind her what she owed him and what he should be able to hope for and expect from her faithfulness.

The muslin, brightened up by the colour of the half unrolled ribbons, lay like a Christmas present on the little table; the position of the lights enhanced the lustre of the gift, all was in order when old Barbara heard Mariane's feet on the steps and hurried to meet her. But with what surprise did she step back when the little female officer rushed past her without noticing her demonstrations of affection, entered the room with unusual haste and movement, threw her feathered hat and dagger on to the table, walked agitatedly up and down, and did not cast a glance on the solemnly lit lights.

'What is it, darling?' the old woman cried out with surprise. 'For heaven's sake, child, what's wrong? Just look at these presents! Whoever could have given them if not your fondest admirer? Norberg is sending you the muslin for a nightdress; he will soon be here himself; he seems to me to be more zealous in his attentions and more open-handed than ever.'

The old woman moved round and was intending to show the gifts, in which she herself had also been considered, when Mariane turned away from the presents and called out passionately: 'Away, away with them! Today I don't want to hear any more about all this; I obeyed you, it was your wish, let it be so! When Norberg returns, I shall once more belong to him and to you, and you can do what you like with me; but until then I want to lead my own life, and even if you had a thousand tongues, you would not talk me out of my plan. I want to give my whole self to the man who loves me and whom I love. Don't make faces! I wish to submit to this passion as if it should last eternally.'

There was no lack of contrary ideas and reasons on the old woman's part; but when she became vehement and bitter in the continuing altercation Mariane jumped up and seized hold of her in front. The old woman laughed excessively loudly. 'I shall have to see to it that you are put into long clothes again', she exclaimed, 'if I am to be sure of my life. Away, get changed! I hope as a girl you will apologize to me for the injury inflicted on me by yourself as a fugitive young gentleman; off with the coat, and the other things! It's an uncomfortable outfit and one that's dangerous for you, as I perceive. The shoulder ribbons are carrying you away with enthusiasm.'

The old woman had placed her hand upon her, but Mariane tore herself away. 'Not so fast!' she cried out, 'I'm expecting another visitor this evening.'

'That's not a good thing,' the old woman interjected. 'Surely not the young, fond, unfledged son of the merchant?' 'The very person,' replied Mariane.

'It seems as if generosity might be becoming your dominant passion,' the old woman answered mockingly: 'You are very keen to make yourself responsible for those under age and those without money! It must be wonderful to be adored as an unselfish donor.'

'You can make fun as much as you wish, I love him! I love him! It is with such delight that I pronounce these words out loud for the first time! That is the passion as I have imagined it so often; it is something of which I earlier had no conception. Yes, I am willing to throw myself at him! I would like to clasp him as if I were going to hold him for ever. I want to show him all my love and to enjoy his love in its whole compass.'

'Calm yourself,' the old woman said quietly, 'Calm yourself! I must interrupt your joy with *one* thought: Norberg is coming!

He's coming in a fortnight. Here is his letter, which came with the presents.'

'And even if the morning sun were to rob me of my friend, I would want to conceal it from myself! A fortnight! What an eternity! What cannot happen in a fortnight, what changes there can be!'

Wilhelm came in. With what liveliness did she fly towards him! With what rapture he embraced the red uniform and pressed the little white waistcoat against his breast! Who would venture to describe the bliss of two people in love, for whom would it be appropriate to make such a declaration! The old woman went to one side grumbling; we depart with her, leaving the happy pair to themselves.

Chapter Two

When Wilhelm greeted his mother next morning she told him that his father was very annoyed and would very soon forbid him to pay daily visits to the theatre. 'Even though I occasionally like to go to the theatre myself,' she continued, 'I am all the same often inclined to curse it, since my domestic quiet is disturbed by your excessive passion for this form of entertainment. Father always asks what use it can be and how can people waste their time with it.'

'I've already had to listen to him as well,' replied Wilhelm, 'And perhaps I answered him too hastily; but for heaven's sake, Mother, is everything useless which does not immediately put money in our pockets and which does not procure us possessions near at hand? Didn't we have room enough in the old house? And was it necessary to build a new one? Doesn't Father spend a considerable part of his business profits in embellishing the rooms? Aren't these silk tapestries and English furnishings also useless? Could we not content ourselves with less? I at least admit that these decorated walls, flowers, flourishes, little baskets and figures repeated a hundred times make a wholly disagreeable impression. At the best they appear to me like our theatre curtain. But how different it is to be sitting in front of this! Even though you may have to wait a long time, you do know that it will be raised, and we shall then see the most varied things which will entertain, enlighten and elevate us.'

'Do take things calmly,' his mother said. 'Father also likes his relaxation in the evening; and then he believes that you will find it entertaining and in the end, if he gets cross, it's my fault. How often have I had to listen to reproaches about the wretched puppet-theatre which I gave you for Christmas twelve years ago and which first gave you a taste for plays!'

'Don't attack the puppet-theatre, don't have any regrets for your love and care! These were the first pleasurable moments which I enjoyed in the new, empty house; I can still picture this moment for myself, I know how strange it seemed to me when, after receiving the usual Christmas presents, we were told to sit down in front of a door which led from another room. The door opened, but not for going to and fro in the usual way; the entrance was filled with an unexpectedly festive atmosphere. A portal was built up high which had been covered by a mysterious curtain. At first we all stood at a distance, and as we became more curious to see what gleaming and rattling things might be concealed behind the half-translucent covering, each one of us was provided with his little chair and asked to wait patiently.

'So now everyone was sitting quietly; there was a whistle as signal, the curtain was raised and revealed a prospect of a temple, painted bright-red. The high priest Samuel appeared with Jonathan, and their alternating, unusual voices seemed to me most venerable. Shortly afterwards Saul came on the scene, much embarrassed because of the impertinence of the huge warrior who had challenged him and his man. How happy I felt when the dwarf-like son of Jesse skipped up with shepherd's staff and pouch, and a sling, and said: "Oh most powerful king and lord, let no one lose courage on this account; if Your Majesty will allow me, I will go forward and engage in conflict with the mighty giant."—The first act was ended, and the audience was very keen to see what would happen further; everyone wished that the music would soon stop. At last the curtain was raised again. David dedicated the monster's flesh to the birds of the air and the animals of the field; the Philistine spoke scornfully, stamped a lot with both feet, fell down finally like a log and gave the whole business a magnificent turning of the scales. When afterwards the maidens sang: "Saul hath slain his thousands, and David his ten thousands," and the giant's head was carried in front of the little conqueror and he received the king's beautiful daughter as his bride, I felt annoyed in spite of all happiness that the lucky prince was so dwarf-shaped. For, following the idea of the great Goliath and the little David, the opportunity had not been missed to make both figures truly characteristic. Please, do you know what has happened to the puppets? I've promised to show them to a friend whom I gave a great deal of pleasure by talking to him recently about this children's entertainment.'

'I'm not surprised that you remember these things so vividly: for it was you who straightaway became the most involved in them. I recall how you took the little book off me and learned the whole play off by heart; I was not aware of this until one evening you made a David and Goliath with wax, got them both to speechify to one another, gave the giant a push finally and fixed his unwieldy head on a big pin with a waxen knob in little David's hand. At that time I took such heartfelt motherly pleasure at your good memory and your lofty talk that I at once determined to hand over the wooden troupe to you myself. I didn't think that it would cause me so many tiresome hours.'

'You mustn't have any regrets,' Wilhelm answered; 'for these amusements have brought us many a happy hour.'

And with these words he asked for the keys, hurried away, found the puppets and for a moment was transported into those times when they had still seemed alive to him, and when he had believed that he could bring them to life with the vivacity of his voice and the movement of his hands. He took them with him to his room and kept them carefully.

Chapter Three

If first love, as I have generally heard maintained, is the most beautiful thing that a heart can feel, whether earlier or later, we must praise our hero as triply happy because it was granted to him to enjoy the bliss of these unique moments in its whole range. Only a few are favoured so pre-eminently, while most people are led away from their earlier feelings only through a hard school in which after scanty enjoyment they are compelled to forego their most ardent wishes and to learn permanently to do without what appeared in their mind's as the greatest happiness.

Wilhelm's yearning for the attractive girl had risen on the wings of imagination; after knowing her a short while he had won her affection, and he found himself in possession of someone whom he loved, indeed adored, so very much: for she had appeared to him first in the favourable light of a theatre performance, and his passion for the stage combined with his first love for a woman. His youth allowed him to partake in rich joys that were enhanced and maintained by a lively imagination. The circumstances of his beloved also gave her behaviour a quality of mood that very much supported his own emotions; the fear that her lover might discover the rest of her affairs prematurely gave her an attractive appearance of worry and shame, her passion for him was intense, even her uneasiness seemed to increase her fondness; she was the most delightful creature in his arms.

When he awakened from the first ecstasy of joy and looked back on his life and his situation, everything seemed new to him, his obligations seemed more solemn, his inclinations keener, his knowledge clearer, his intentions firmer. Consequently it became easy for him to make an arrangement which would allow him to escape his father's reproaches, to calm his mother down, and to enjoy Mariane's love in an untroubled manner. During the day he got on with his business punctually, usually did without going to the theatre, made conversation at table in the evening, and when everyone was in bed he slipped quietly out to the garden wrapped in his cloak, and hurried impetuously to his beloved, his heart full of romantic thoughts.

'What have you got there?' Mariane asked, when one evening he brought out a bundle which the old woman, in the hope of agreeable presents, looked at very attentively. 'You'll never guess', Wilhelm replied.

How surprised was Mariane and how horrified was Barbara when the serviette was untied and revealed a confused heap of puppets, each the length of the span of a hand. Mariane laughed out loud when Wilhelm made efforts to separate the tangled wires and to point to each figure separately. The old woman crept to one side, irritated.

It only needs something slight to entertain two lovers, and so our friends were very well pleased that evening. The little troupe was mustered, each figure closely examined and laughed at. Mariane refused to take pleasure in King Saul in black velvet robe with golden crown; he looked too stiff and pedantic for her, she said. All the more did Jonathan please her, with his smooth chin, his yellow and red dress and his turban. What is more, she could turn him neatly this way and that by means of the wire, make him bow and cause him to make declarations of love. On the other hand, she was reluctant to pay the prophet Samuel the least attention, even though Wilhelm sang the praises of the little breastplate and recounted that the shot taffeta of the frock-coat came from an old dress of his grandmother. David was too small for her and Goliath too big; she held firm to her Jonathan. She knew how to act so agreeably with him and in the end to transfer her caresses from the puppet to our friend that again this time a commonplace game became the introduction to hours of happiness.

They were aroused from the sweetness of their fond dreams by a noise that arose in the street. Mariane called the old woman who, still busy as was her custom, was occupied at adjusting the variable equipment of the theatre wardrobe for use in the next play. She provided the information that a company of merry-makers was just staggering out of the Italian Cellar close by where they had not been sparing of the champagne with their fresh, newly arrived oysters.

'A pity,' said Mariane 'that we didn't think about it earlier, we too might have indulged ourselves.'

'I expect there's still time,' Wilhelm rejoined, handing the old woman a louis d'or; 'if you get what we want, you can partake with us'.

The old woman was nimble, and in a short time an agreeably laid table with a well arranged collation stood before the lovers. The old woman had to sit at the table too; they ate, drank and enjoyed themselves.

On such occasions there was no lack of conversational material. Mariane brought out her Jonathan again, and the old woman was able to turn the conversation to Wilhelm's favourite subject. 'You have already entertained us once with an account of the first performance of a puppet-play on Christmas Eve; it was jolly to hear about. You were just interrupted when the ballet was due to start. Now we have met the magnificent cast that achieved those great effects.'

'Yes,' said Mariane, 'go on with the story, how did you feel?'

'It is a beautiful feeling, dear Mariane,' Wilhelm replied, 'when we remember old times and old, harmless mistakes, particularly if it happens at a moment when we have been fortunate enough to reach a high point from which we can look around and survey the path by which we have come. It is so pleasant to have a complacent memory of a number of obstacles which we often used to think of with a feeling of embarrassment as insurmountable, and to compare how we have now developed with what we were like then in an undeveloped state. But now I feel inexpressibly happy, as I talk with you at this moment about the past, because at the same time I am looking ahead to the delightful country which we can wander through together hand in hand.'

'How about the ballet?' the old woman interposed. 'I have a fear that everything did not proceed as it should have done.'

'Oh yes,' Wilhelm rejoined, 'very well! A vague memory of those strange leaps of negroes and negresses, shepherds and shepherdesses, and dwarf men and women has remained in my mind for the whole of my life. Then the curtain fell, the door closed, and the entire little group hurried off to bed, as if drunk and staggering; but I do know that I couldn't go to sleep, that I asked for a further story to be told me, that I still put a lot of questions and that it was only with reluctance that I let the nurse-maid go who had settled us down in bed.

'The magic structure had unfortunately disappeared again the next morning, the mysterious curtain had been removed, it was again possible to move freely through that particular door from one room to the other, and so many adventurous happenings had left no trace. My brothers and sisters ran this way and that with their toys, I alone went creeping up and down, it seemed impossible to me that there should only be a couple of door-posts where yesterday there had been so much magic. Ah, he who looks for a lost love cannot be unhappier than I appeared to myself at that time!'

A glance that was intoxicated with joy, which he cast upon Mariane, convinced her that he did not fear that he might ever get into that position.

Chapter Four

'My one wish now,' Wilhelm continued, 'was to see a second performance of the play. I entreated my mother, and she endeavoured to persuade my father at an opportune moment; but her effort was in vain. He maintained that a rarely experienced pleasure could acquire value for people, and that children and old people did not know how to esteem good things that came their way every day.

'Indeed, we should have to wait a long time still, perhaps until Christmas came again, if the constructor and secret director of the show had not himself felt the desire to repeat the performance and along with this to produce in an epilogue a harlequin figure that had been very recently completed.

'A young artilleryman, endowed with many talents and particularly skilful in mechanical tasks, who had performed many important services to Father during the building work and who had been amply recompensed by him, wanted to express his gratitude to the little family at Christmas time and presented to the house of his patron this completely furnished theatre which he had constructed, carved and painted during idle hours at an earlier time. It was he, with the help of a servant, who worked the puppets himself and who spoke the various parts with a disguised voice. It was not difficult for him to persuade Father, who conceded to a friend as a favour what he had refused his children as a matter of conviction. Enough—the theatre was once more set up, a few of the neighbours' children asked in and the play repeated.

'If on the first occasion I had experienced the joy of surprise and astonishment, it was the pleasure of attention and investigation that dominated the second. *How* it worked was now my concern. I had already said to myself the first time that the puppets did not speak themselves; I also conjectured that they did not move of their own accord; but why was it all so attractive none the less? And yet why did it look as if they were speaking and moving themselves? And where might the lights and the people be? These enigmas disturbed me all the more, the more I wished to be at the same time among those who were enchanted and among the magicians, both to have a hand in the play and be a spectator enjoying the pleasure of the illusion.

'The play was over, preparations were being made for the epilogue, the spectators had got up and were chatting amongst themselves. I pressed closer to the door and heard from the clattering inside that people were busy clearing up. I lifted up the lower tapestry and peeped between the framework. My mother noticed it and pulled me back; however, I had seen this much, that friends and foes, Saul and Goliath and the rest of them, were being packed into one drawer, and so my half-satisfied curiosity received fresh stimulus. At the same time I was most astonished to see the lieutenant being very busy in the holy of holies. Now Harlequin, however much he clattered with his heels, could not keep me entertained. I became lost in deep thought and after this discovery became both calmer and less calm than before. After I had learnt something, it began to seem to me as if I knew nothing, and I was right: for I did not see the connection, and after all this is the whole point.'

Chapter Five

'In well arranged and orderly houses,' Wilhelm continued, 'the children have a feeling similar to that experienced by rats and mice; they pay attention to any chinks and holes by means of which they can have access to forbidden sweets; they enjoy these with a great deal of stealthy voluptuous fear, which comprises such a large part of childish happiness.

'I was more attentive than any of my brothers and sisters whenever a key was left in a lock. The greater the reverence was which I carried around in my heart for locked doors, which I had to pass by for weeks and months on end and into which I could only occasionally cast a furtive glance when Mother opened the sanctuary in order to take something out, the quicker I was to make use of a moment which the carelessness of housekeepers on various occasions caused to occur.

'As may easily be imagined, of all doors it was the door of the pantry to which my senses were most sharply directed. Few of life's anticipatory joys could compare with the feeling I had when my mother called on me from time to time to help her carry something out, and I then owed a debt of gratitude either to her goodness or to my cunning for a few prunes. The heaped-up treasures embraced my imagination with their abundance, and even the strange smell exhaled by so many kinds of spices in confusion made an impression of such tastiness on me that I never neglected, whenever I was nearby, at least to gloat at the atmosphere revealed there. This noteworthy key was left in the lock one Sunday morning when Mother had been overtaken by the ringing of bells and the whole house lay in a deep Sabbath calm. No sooner had I noticed it, when I walked gently up and down a few times, pressed quietly and artfully close, opened the door and with *one* step felt myself close to so much long-desired bliss. I cast a quick, doubting glance upon coffers, sacks, boxes, cases and jars, to see what I should select and take, in the end seized hold of the beloved prunes, provided myself with some dried apples and, modestly enough, took in addition a piece of candied orangepeel; I was about to slither backwards again with this booty when I noticed a few boxes standing side by side, from one of which wires provided with hooks at the top were hanging out because of the badly closed bolt. I fell upon this with premonitory feelings; and with what unworldly emotion did I discover that my world of heroes and happiness was stacked up there. I was going to lift up and look at the ones on top, and pull out those at the bottom; but I very soon entangled the delicate wires and got myself into a state of uneasiness and anxiety, especially as the cook made some movements in the nearby kitchen, so that I pressed everything together as well as I could, bolted the box, only taking out for myself a booklet that had lain on top and which contained the comedy of David and Goliath, and made my escape with this booty quietly up the stairs into an attic.

'From this time on I spent all my secret, solitary hours in repeatedly reading my play, learning it off by heart and thinking to myself how magnificent it would be, if I could also give the figures life with my fingers. In my thoughts I became David and Goliath myself in the process. I studied the play and absorbed it into my being in all corners of the attic, stables and gardens, in all kinds of circumstances, I took possession of all roles and learnt them by heart, except that I usually placed myself in the part of the hero and left the rest of the characters to jog along in my memory only as followers. So David's magnanimous speeches, with which he challenged the arrogant giant Goliath, haunted me night and day; I often murmured them aloud, but nobody paid any attention except Father who occasionally noticed some exclamation and commended to himself the good memory of his boy who had been able to remember such a lot after so little listening.

'Because of this I became bolder and bolder, and one evening recited most of the play to my mother, while moulding for myself a few pieces of wax as actors. She became alert, was insistent with me, and I confessed.

'Fortunately this discovery took place at a time when the lieutenant himself had expressed the wish to be allowed to initiate me into these secrets. My mother at once told him about the unexpected talent of her son, and he was able to arrange for a few rooms on the top floor which were usually empty to be put at his disposal; in one of them once more the audience was to sit, in the other the players and the proscenium should again fill up the doorway. Father had allowed his friend to arrange all this, while he himself only appeared to look on tolerantly, following the principle that one should not let children notice how fond one was of them, or else they would take liberties; he believed that one had to seem to be serious when they were enjoying themselves and occasionally to spoil their pleasures so that their contentment should not make them immoderate and presumptuous.'

Chapter Six

'The lieutenant now put up the theatre and looked after the other things. I noticed indeed that he came into the house several times during the week and surmised the purpose. My eagerness grew incredibly, as I certainly felt that I should not be allowed to take any part before Saturday in what was being prepared. At last the longed-for day arrived. My guide came at five in the afternoon and took me up with him. Trembling with joy I stepped inside and saw on both sides of the frame the puppets hanging down in the order in which they were to appear; I examined them carefully, ascended the step which raised me above the theatre, so that now I was hovering over the little world. I looked down between the boards not without reverence, because I was in the grip of the memory of the magnificent effect which the whole had from the outside, and was sensitive what secrets were being revealed to me. We had one try, and it went well.

'Next day, when a group of children were invited, we managed very well, except that in the heat of the moment I dropped Jonathan and was compelled to put my hand down to pick him up: a mischance that destroyed the illusion very much, caused great laughter and wounded my feelings unutterably. This slip also seemed to be very welcome to Father, who with circumspection refused to reveal the great pleasure he obtained from seeing his little son so capable, and immediately picked on the mistakes when the play was over, saying it would have been really nice, if only this and that had not gone wrong.

'I was deeply hurt, I became sad for the rest of the evening, but by the next morning I had already slept off all ill humour again and was blissful in thinking that I had performed excellently, apart from the mishap. Added to this was the applause of the spectators who emphatically maintained that although the lieutenant had done a great deal in the use of rough and refined voices, none the less his perorations were mostly too affected and stiff; on the other hand the new beginner rendered his David and Jonathan very well; Mother in particular praised the candid manner in which I had challenged Goliath and introduced the modest victor to the king.

'Now, to my great joy, the theatre remained set up, and as spring was coming and it was possible to manage without a fire, I stayed in the attic in my free time and my play periods and had the puppets performing in sturdy confusion together. I often asked my brothers and sisters and friends to come up; but even when they didn't want to come, I was up there on my own. My imagination brooded over the little world, which quite soon assumed another form.

'No sooner had I performed the first play, for which theatre and actors had been created and primed, a few times than it already ceased to give me any pleasure. However, the *German Stage*[1] and various Italian-German operas, which were among Grandfather's books, had come into my hands; I became engrossed in these and each time only reckoned up the number of personages in advance and then proceeded without further ado to the performance of the play. And now King Saul in his black velvet robe had to play Chaumigrem, Cato and Darius; at this point it may be noted that the plays were never performed completely, but for the most part only the fifth acts, where the slaughtering took place.

'It was also natural that opera with its multifarious transformations and adventures would attract me above all. Here I could find stormy seas, gods descending in clouds, and what made me particularly happy, thunder and lightning. I assisted myself with cardboard, paint and paper, could produce a first-class night, the lightning looked really terrifying, it was only that the thunder did not always work, but that didn't matter all that much. What is more, the operas offered more opportunity to bring on David and Goliath, which couldn't be managed at all in ordinary drama. Every day I felt more attachment to the narrow little seat where I had so much enjoyment; and I admit that the smell which the puppets had acquired from the pantry contributed not a little to this.

'The scenery for my theatre was now fairly complete; for it now proved very useful that from an early age onwards I had had a talent for handling compasses, cutting out cardboard and illuminating pictures. It upset me all the more when the servants quite often hindered me in the execution of great achievements.

'My sisters, when dressing and undressing their dolls, stimulated in me the idea of gradually providing my heroes also with clothes that could be changed. The bits of clothing were separated from their bodies and put together as well as could be managed, new ribbon and finery was bought with money saved, many a piece of taffeta was procured by begging, and gradually a theatre wardrobe was collected in which farthingales for the ladies had not been forgotten.

1. *The German Stage (Deutsche Schaubühne)* 'arranged according to the rules of the ancient Greeks and Romans', a collection of plays compiled by J. C. Gottsched from 1740-45. (Tr.)

'The troupe was really provided now with clothes for a play on the largest scale, and one would have thought that now in fact one performance would follow the other; but it happened to me as it often happens to children; they conceive far-reaching plans, make ambitious arrangements, indeed a few attempts too, and then everything is left. I must also indict myself of this failing. For me the greatest joy lay in discovery and in the occupation of the imagination. This play or the other aroused my interest because of a particular scene, and at once I again had new clothes made for it. As a result of these ventures the original costumes of my heroes had got into disarray and had been mislaid, so that not even the first big play could be performed any more. I let my imagination take over, was eternally rehearsing and making preparations, built a thousand castles in the air, and did not realize that I had destroyed the foundation of the little building.'

Throughout this narrative Mariane had exercised all her fondness for Wilhelm to conceal her sleepiness. Amusing as the happening might seem from one point of view, it really was too simple as far as she was concerned, and the comments about it too ponderous. Tenderly she placed her foot on the foot of her beloved and gave him apparent indications of her attention and approval. She drank from his glass, and Wilhelm was convinced that no word of his account had been lost. After a short pause he exclaimed: 'Now it's your turn, Mariane, to tell me about your early childhood pleasures. Up to now we have always been too preoccupied with what is happening now for us to have been able to concern ourselves mutually with our earlier ways of life. Tell me: under what conditions were you brought up? What are the first vivid impressions you remember?'

These questions would have greatly embarrassed Mariane, if the old woman had not at once come to her aid. 'Do you believe, then,' the shrewd woman said, 'that we pay so much attention to what happened to us at an early stage that we have such agreeable incidents to relate, and if we did have them to relate, that we should also be able to present them with such skill?'

'As if that were necessary!' Wilhelm cried out. 'I love this sweet, good, dear creature so much that I resent every moment of my life which I have spent without her. Let me at least take part in your past life in my imagination! Tell me all, and I will tell you all. Let us deceive ourselves wherever possible and try to regain those times that have been lost for love.'

'If you insist so eagerly, we can satisfy you, I'm sure,' the old woman said. 'Only tell us first how your enthusiasm for the theatre gradually grew, what practice you had, how you improved to such an extent that you can now be considered to be a good actor. Certainly, there won't have been any lack of entertaining incidents. It is not worth our while to go to sleep now, I have another bottle in reserve; and who knows when we are able to sit quietly and contentedly together again?'

Mariane looked up to her with a sad glance, which Wilhelm did not notice, and he continued in his narrative.

Chapter Seven

'As my circle of comrades began to increase, the distractions of youth were detrimental to solitary and quiet pleasures. I was by turns hunter, soldier or rider, as our games required; but I always had one small advantage over the others in being able to construct skilfully the necessary implements. Thus the swords were mostly of my manufacture, it was I who decorated and gilded the sledges, and a deep-rooted instinct would not let me rest until I had remodelled our militia in the classical style. Helmets were constructed, decorated with paper plumes, shields, even suits of armour were made, labours over which the household servants who happened to be skilled tailors, and the seamstresses broke many a needle.

'Some of my young companions I now saw well arrayed, the others were also equipped gradually, though to a lesser extent, and a splendid corps was formed. We marched about in yards and gardens, bravely gave each other blows on shields and heads; there were plenty of disagreements, but they were soon settled.

'This game, which greatly entertained the others, had only been played a few times when it ceased to satisfy me. The sight of so many armed figures stimulated in me ideas about knights which had been filling my head for some time, as I had started reading old romances.

'Jerusalem Delivered, of which Kopp's translation came my way, at last gave my rambling thoughts a definite direction. It is true, I could not read the poem in its entirety; but there were passages which I knew by heart and whose images haunted me. In particular everything about Clorinda fascinated me. The amazon-like quality and quiet completeness of her existence had more effect on a mind that was beginning to develop than the artificial charms of Armida, although I did not despise her garden.

'But hundreds and hundreds of times when I walked in the evenings on the balcony which is placed between the house gables, when I looked out over the district, when a trembling light from the disappearing sun was visible on the horizon, when the stars came forth, when night emerged from all angles and depths, and the chirping of the crickets sounded shrilly through the solemn stillness, did I recite the story of the sad duel between Tancred and Clorinda.

'However much I was on the Christians' side, as was proper, I none the less supported the pagan heroine with my whole heart when she undertook to set fire to the great tower of the besiegers. And the way Tancred now meets the supposed warrior at night, the dispute begins under the cover of darkness and they fight fiercely—I could never pronounce the words:

> Yet now the measure of Clorinda's life is high
> And so the hour draws near when she is doomed to die!

without the tears coming into my eyes and flowing profusely as the unhappy lover plunges the sword into her breast, recognizes her and tremulously fetches water to baptize her.

'But how my heart was moved when Tancred's sword strikes the tree in the enchanted forest, blood flows after the blow has been dealt, and a voice resounds in his ears telling him that here too he is wounding Clorinda, that he is destined by fate to injure what he loves wherever he goes and without knowing!

'The story so took possession of my imagination that what I had read of the poem formed itself in my mind to a whole which captivated me so much that I thought of performing it in some way or other. I wanted to play Tancred and Rinaldo, and I found that two sets of armour which I had already prepared were quite ready for this purpose. The one made of dark-grey paper with scales was to adorn the serious-minded Tancred, the other with its silver and gold paper was to embellish the splendid Rinaldo. In the liveliness of my conception I told everything to my friends who were much delighted by it, only they could not really understand that it was all to be performed, and what is more, performed by themselves.

'I overcame these doubts with great readiness, I immediately believed I could count on a few rooms in a neighbouring playmate's house, without envisaging that the old aunt would never release them; the same applied to the theatre, concerning which I also had no definite ideas, except that it had to be set up on joists, that wings out of divided folding screens had to be put in position and that a big cloth was necessary for the floor. But where the materials and implements were to come from, I had not considered.

'We found a good source of supply for the forest: we spoke politely to an old servant of one of the houses, who had now become a forester, to ask him to get hold of young birches and pines for us, and in fact they were brought along more speedily than we could have hoped for. But now we were in the awkward situation of how to put the play on before the trees withered. This was a critical situation; we lacked a site, a theatre and curtains. The folding screens were the only things we had.

'In this embarrassment we once more turned to the lieutenant for whom we provided a lengthy description of the magnificence which was to be forthcoming. Although he understood us only dimly, he was very helpful, he pushed together into a little room whatever tables could be found in the house and the neighbourhood, put the screens on them, made a rear view of green curtains, while the trees were also brought in and put in a row.

'Meanwhile it had become evening, the lights had been lit, the maids and the children were sitting in their seats, the play was due to start, and the whole band of heroes was dressed up; but now everyone felt for the first time that he did not know what he had to say. In the heat of my inventiveness I had forgotten what after all everybody has to know, that is, what he has to say and when he has to say it; and in the excitement of the construction activity it had not occurred to the others either; they believed they could easily perform as heroes, easily act and talk like the personages in whose world I had put them. They all stood in astonishment, asking each other what was to come first, and I, who had thought of myself as Tancred from the start, began to recite a few lines from the epic, having appeared on my own. But because the passage only too soon continued in narrative style and I finally appeared in my own speech in the third person, and because Godfrey, the subject of the speech, refused to appear, I simply had to walk off again, amid the loud laughter of my audience: a mishap that hurt me deeply. The enterprise had come to grief; the audience was sitting there and wanted to see something. We were dressed up; I pulled myself together and in short decided to play David and Goliath. Some of the company had performed the puppet-play with me of old, they had all often seen it; the parts were handed out, everybody promised to do their best, and a funny small lad painted a black beard on himself, so that, if a gap should appear he could fill it as Harlequin with a farcical episode; an occurrence which I was very reluctant to allow, as I considered it to be contrary to the seriousness of the play. However, I vowed that, once I had escaped from the present embarrassment, I would never venture upon the performance of a play without the maturest consideration.'

Chapter Eight

Mariane, overcome by sleep, leaned against her beloved who pressed her firmly to him and continued in his narrative, while the old woman enjoyed with careful reflection what was left of the wine.

'We soon forgot the embarrassment in which I and my friends had found ourselves when we undertook to perform a non-existent play. Even the most recalcitrant material could not resist my passion to depict in a play every novel which I read, every story that was taught me. I was fully convinced that everything that was entertaining as a story would have to have a much greater effect if put on the stage; everything was to happen before my eyes, on the stage. When we had lessons in world history at school, I carefully marked out the place where someone had been stabbed to death or poisoned in a particular manner, and hastened on to the interesting fifth act. In this way I really did start to write some plays in a back-to-front manner, without my coming as far as the beginning even in one single case.

'At the same time I read through a whole chaotic collection of output for the theatre, just as chance put it into my hands; I did this partly on my own initiative and partly at the suggestion of my good friends who had taken a fancy to acting plays. I was at that happy age when we still take pleasure in everything, when we find our satisfaction in quantity and variety. Unfortunately, however, my judgment was corrupted in yet another way. Those plays particularly pleased me in which I hoped to make a good impression, and there were few which I did not read through with this agreeable deception in mind, and my lively imagination misled me to the belief that, since I could think myself into all roles, I would also perform them all; therefore when parts were being decided on, I usually chose those which were not at all suitable for me, and if at all possible, preferably several parts.

'Children when playing know how to make anything do for any purpose: a stick becomes a gun, a bit of wood a dagger, any little bundle becomes a doll and any corner a cottage. It was in this sense that our private theatre developed. Being fully unaware of what powers we might or might not have, we tackled anything, did not notice any *qui pro quo,* and were convinced that everybody must take us for what we claimed to be. Unfortunately it all took place in such an ordinary way, that I can't even recall any striking piece of silliness that might be reported. First we went through the few plays in which only male characters appear; then we dressed up some from our group, and finally we brought our sisters into the game. In some houses it was considered a useful occupation, and groups of people were asked in. Here again our artillery lieutenant did not desert us. He showed us how we should walk on and walk off, how we should declaim and gesticulate; though for the most part he was given little thanks for his efforts, as we thought that we already understood the theatre arts better than he did.

'We soon came on to tragedy: for we had often heard it said and we believed ourselves that it was easier to write and enact a tragedy than to be perfect in comedy. What was more, at our first attempt at tragedy we felt wholly in our element; we tried to approach elevation in class and excellence of character by means of stiffness and affectation, and had quite an opinion of ourselves; but we were only really happy when we could rave, stamp our feet, and indeed throw ourselves on to the ground in rage and despair.

'These games had not brought boys and girls together for long before nature began to stir and the company started to split up into various little love-affairs, as for the most part comedy was being played within the comedy. The happy couples held hands most fondly behind the theatre screens; they were full of bliss whenever they could appear to one another, with their ribbons and finery, in a really idealized light, while confronting them the unhappy rivals were consumed with envy, and defiantly and gloatingly instigated all kinds of mischief.

'Although undertaken without understanding and carried out without guidance, these games were none the less not without use to us. We exercised our memories and our bodies, and attained more suppleness in speech and manners than it is usually possible to acquire at such a youthful stage. But for me that time was particularly momentous, my mind was directed wholly to the theatre, and I knew no greater happiness than to be reading and writing plays and to be acting in them.

'My teachers' instruction continued, I was to be placed in the world of commerce and was assigned to our neighbour's counting-house; but just at that very time my spirit felt only the more forcefully separated from everything that I was constrained to consider as a base occupation. I wanted to dedicate my whole activity to the stage, to find there my happiness and contentment.

'I can still remember a poem, which must be among my papers somewhere, in which the muse of tragic poetry and another female figure, in which I had personified commerce, quarrel really thoroughly over my esteemed person. The invention is commonplace, and I don't recall whether the verse is very good; but you ought to have a look at it for the sake of the fear, disgust, love and passion which predominate there. What a fearful figure I had portrayed in the old housewife, with the distaff in her sash, keys at her side, and glasses on her nose, always busy, always in a commotion, quarrelsome and thrifty, petty and importunate! How wretched was the condition, as I described it, of the man who was to bow beneath her rod and to perform his menial daily task by the sweat of his brow!

'How differently the other figure appeared by contrast! What a vision she became to the careworn heart! Magnificently formed, to be seen in her nature and behaviour as a daughter of freedom. Her awareness of her value gave her dignity without pride; her clothes were appropriate, they enveloped each limb without constraining it, and the ample folds of the material reiterated like a thousandfold echo the charming movements of the divine personage. What a contrast! And to which side my heart turned, you can easily imagine. Nor was anything forgotten to make my muse recognizable. Crowns and daggers, chains and masks, as they had been handed down to me by my predecessors, had been allocated to her here too. The contest was intense, the speeches of both figures were suitably contrasted, since someone in his fourteenth year is usually accustomed to painting black and white really close together. The old woman talked as would be appropriate in someone who picks up a pin, and the other one like someone who is going to give away a kingdom. The warning threats of the old woman were despised; I had already turned my back on the riches promised to me: disinherited and denuded, I committed myself to the muse, who threw me her golden veil and covered my nakedness.

'If I had been able to conceive, o my darling!' he exclaimed, clasping Mariane closely to himself, 'that a quite different, more lovable divinity would come, and strengthen me in my resolution and accompany me on my way—what a more beautiful turning-point my poem would have taken, how interesting would its conclusion have been! But what I find in your arms is no poem, it is truth and life; let us enjoy the sweet happiness in full awareness!'

Mariane had been awakened by the pressure of his arm and the liveliness of his raised voice, and hid her embarrassment in caresses; for she had not heard a word of the last part of his narrative, and it is to be wished that our hero may find in future more attentive listeners to his favourite stories.

Chapter Nine

In this way Wilhelm spent his nights in the enjoyment of intimate love, and his days in the expectation of further blissful hours. Already at the time when desire and hope had been drawing him to Mariane, he felt as if given new life, he felt that he was beginning to become another man; now he had been united with her, the satisfaction of his wishes was becoming a delightful habit. His heart was striving to ennoble the object of his passions, his mind was aiming to raise up the beloved girl along with himself. The thought of her preoccupied him during the shortest absence. If she had previously been necessary to him, now she was indispensable, as he was tied to her by all the bonds of humanity. His pure soul felt that she was half, more than half, of himself. He was thankful and devoted without limits.

Mariane too was able to deceive herself for a time; she shared the feeling of his spirited happiness with him. Oh, if only the cold hand of self-reproach had not at times passed over her heart! Even in Wilhelm's arms she was not safe from it, even beneath the wings of his love. And when she was once more on her own, having come down from the clouds, where his passion transported her, into consciousness of her circumstances, she was to be pitied. For thoughtlessness came to her aid as long as she lived in obscure confusion and deceived herself about her circumstances, or rather did not know them; then the happenings to which she had been exposed only appeared to her singly: pleasure and annoyance alternated, humiliation was compensated by vanity, and want often by momentary superfluity; she could cite to herself necessity and habit as law and justification, and for a time all unpleasant feelings could be shaken off from hour to hour, from day to day. Now, however, the poor girl had felt that she had been moved into a better world for moments, she had looked down, as if from above, from light and joy to the dismal and base element of her life, she had felt what a wretched creature a woman is who does not arouse love and respect as well as desire, and she found that she had improved not at all, whether outwardly or inwardly. She had nothing which could uplift and comfort her. When she looked within herself and sought, her mind was empty and her heart had no support. The sadder this condition grew, the more intensively did her inclination hold tightly to the beloved, just as the danger of losing him came closer every day.

Wilhelm, on the other hand, was poised happily in higher regions, for him too a new world had been revealed, but one that was rich in wonderful prospects. Scarcely was there a lessening of the excess of first happiness, when he could see clearly in his soul what had hitherto been running through his mind in an obscure manner. 'She is yours! She has given herself to you! She, the dear creature who had been sought after and worshipped, has given herself to you in full trust; but she has not put herself in the hands of someone who is ungrateful.' Wherever he was, he would be talking to himself; his heart continually overflowed, and in a plethora of splendid words he recited to himself the noblest sentiments. He believed he could see the clear indication of fate that was through Mariane offering him its hand in order to pull him out of the slow, shuffling middle-class way of life, from which he had already wished to escape for a long time. It seemed an easy matter to leave his father's house and his relatives. He was young and new in the world, and his confidence to run after happiness and satisfaction in its lengths and depths had been heightened by love. His destiny for the theatre was now clear to him; the high aim which he saw set up for himself seemed nearer to him as he aspired to Mariane's hand, and in complacent modesty he saw himself as the outstanding actor and creator of a future national theatre, on behalf of whose establishment he had heard so many sigh. Everything that up to now had slumbered in the innermost recesses of his soul became active. From the multifarious ideas he painted with colours of love a picture on a misty ground whose figures, it is true, flowed into one another considerably; but in return for that the whole made all the more charming an impression.

Chapter Ten

He was sitting at home now, rummaging among his papers and preparing for his departure. Whatever recalled his destiny as it had proceeded up to that point was laid aside; in his travels into the world he wanted also to be free from any unpleasant impression. Only works of taste, poets and critics, were placed as familiar friends among the elect; and as up to now he had made very little use of art critics, his eagerness for instruction was rekindled when he once more looked through his books and discovered that the pages of the theoretical writings had for the most part not yet been cut. Fully convinced of the necessity of such works, he had acquired many of them and with the best will in the world had not been able to read more than halfway through any of them.

On the other hand he had held all the more keenly to examples and had himself made attempts in all forms that were known to him.

Werner came in, and when he saw his friend occupied with the familiar exercise-books, he called out: 'Are you yet again concerned with these papers? I'll bet you don't intend to finish any one of them! You'll look through them, and then look them through again, and at most you'll start something new.'

'It isn't up to the pupil to complete something, it's enough if he practices.'

'But nevertheless he should finish it off, as well as he can.'

'And yet the question might well be asked as to whether we should not be truly hopeful of a young person who on realizing when he has started something clumsily, does not continue with the work and does not wish to waste time and energy on something that can never be of value.'

'I do know it was never like you to finish something off, you were always weary before it was half finished. When you were still managing our puppet-shows, how often were new clothes made for the dwarf company, or new scenery cut out? Now this tragedy was to be performed, now that, and the most that it came to was one performance of the fifth act, where there was a lot of confusion and people stabbed each other.'

'If you want to talk about those times, whose fault was it that we removed the clothes that fitted our puppets and were sewn on to their bodies and went to the trouble and expense of an extensive and useless wardrobe? Wasn't it you who always had a new piece of ribbon to sell and who made a point of stimulating me in my hobby and making use of it?'

Werner laughed and exclaimed: 'I still remember with pleasure that I gained advantages from your theatrical campaigns, as contractors do from wars. When you were arming for the liberation of Jerusalem, I made quite a good profit, as the Venetians formerly did in a similar case. I can find nothing on earth more sensible than to take advantage of the follies of others.'

'I don't know whether it would not be a more worthwhile pleasure to cure people of their follies.'

'From what I know of them, this might well be a vain endeavour. Quite an effort is required if one man is to become clever and rich, and for the most part he does so at the expense of others.'

'I've just come across "The Youth at the Crossroads" at the right time,' replied Wilhelm, taking one exercise-book away from the other papers; 'this is one that really was finished, whatever it may be like, by the way.'

'Put it aside, throw it into the fire!' Werner rejoined. 'In its inventiveness it is not in the least praiseworthy; already in earlier days this poem annoyed me and brought your father's disapproval. The poetry may be quite pleasant; but the conception is basically wrong. I can still remember your personification of commerce, your withered and wretched Sibyl. I suppose you picked up the picture in some wretched cheap-jack shop. At that time you had no idea what trade was; I can't think of anyone whose essential nature should be, would have to be, more widely promulgated than that of a genuine business-man. What a panorama is not provided for us by the orderliness in which we pursue our business! It lets us have a conspectus of the whole at any time without our needing to be confused by detail. What advantages are conferred on the trader by double-entry bookkeeping! It is one of the finest inventions of the human spirit, and every good manager should introduce it in his administration.'

'Excuse me,' Wilhelm said with a smile, 'you are starting with the form as if that were the thing itself; but usually you people forget the actual texture of life with all your adding and balancing.'

'Unfortunately you don't see, my friend, how form and content here are one single unit, and how the one could not exist without the other. Order and clarity increase the pleasure in saving and earning. A man who is a bad manager no doubt feels at ease in darkness; he may well be not at all willing to reckon up the items that he owes. On the other hand for a good manager there can be nothing more pleasant than to work out the balance of his growing happiness every day. Even a mishap, if it should surprise and irritate him, will not terrify him; for he knows at once what advantages that he has acquired are to be put in the other pan of the scales. I am convinced, my dear friend, that if you could only acquire a true taste for our business affairs, you would be convinced that here also many of the mind's qualities can develop freely.'

'It's possible that the journey which I am planning will lead me to other thoughts.'

'Oh certainly! Believe me, all that you lack is the prospect of a great piece of activity in order to make you one of us for ever; and when you come back, you will gladly associate yourself with those who, through all kinds of dispatching and speculating, know how to seize for themselves a portion of the money and well-being that make their necessary circulation in the world. Cast a glance on the natural and artificial products of all parts of the globe, see how in turn they have become necessities! What an agreeable, intelligent concern it is to know all the things that are most in demand at a given moment and none the less are sometimes impossible to get, at other times difficult, to be able to provide everybody easily and quickly with what they ask for, to buy up stocks cautiously and to enjoy the advantage of every moment of this great process of circulation! This is something, it seems to me, that will bring great pleasure to anyone who has any sense.'

Wilhelm did not appear disinclined, and Werner went on: 'Just visit a few large business towns, a few harbours, and you will certainly be enthralled as well. When you see how many people are employed, when you see where much of the goods comes from and where it goes, you will surely also be pleased to see it going through your own hands. You will see the smallest piece of merchandise in the context of business as a whole, and for that very reason you will not consider anything as trivial, because everything increases the circulation from which your life derives its nourishment.'

Werner, who was developing his true understanding in his association with Wilhelm, had accustomed himself to think also of his trade and his business with exaltation, and always believed that he could do so with more justification than his otherwise sensible and esteemed friend who, as it seemed to him, placed so much value and threw in the weight of his whole heart upon what was the most unreal thing in the world. He often thought that it could not fail at all, that this false enthusiasm would surely be overcome, and that such a good man could be set on the right road. With this hope in mind he continued: 'The great men of this world have obtained control of this earth, they live in magnificence and superabundance. The smallest area of our continent has already been taken as a possession, each property has been consolidated, official posts and other civic occupations don't bring in much; now where can a more legitimate form of gain or a fairer type of conquest still be found apart from trade? If the princes of this world have the rivers, roads and harbours in their power and make a big profit out of what goes in and through—why should not we seize the opportunity with joy and through our activity likewise exact duty from those whose articles have become indispensable to people partly through need, partly through extravagance? And I can assure you, if only you would apply your poetic imagination, you could boldly present my goddess as an insuperable conqueror of yours. It is true, she prefers to bear the olive branch rather than the sword; she is unacquainted with dagger and chains; but her favourites too receive from her crowns which, let it be said without disparagement of them, glitter with true gold that has been taken from the source and with pearls that she has fetched from the depths of the sea by means of her ever busy servants.'

Wilhelm found this tirade a little tiresome, but he concealed his irritation: for he remembered that Werner usually listened to his harangues too with composure. Incidentally, he was fair-minded enough to be glad to see anyone thinking most highly of his own calling; the only thing was that his own calling, to which he had devoted himself passionately, had to be left undisputed.

'And what a dramatic performance it will be for you, who have such warm sympathy for human affairs,' Werner cried out, 'when you see the happiness that goes with bold undertakings granted to people before your very eyes! What is more attractive than the sight of a ship returning from a prosperous voyage, arriving back before time with a good haul? Not only relations, acquaintances and shareholders, any stranger who happens to be watching feels moved when he sees the joy with which the imprisoned sailor jumps on land even before his vessel is fully in touch with it, feels free again, and can now entrust to the faithful earth what he has removed from the perfidious water. It is not only in figures, my friend, that profit appears to us; fortune is the goddess of living people, and in order truly to feel her favour, we must be alive and see people who make efforts in a really lively manner and can really enjoy life with their senses.'

Chapter Eleven

It is now time for us to become more closely acquainted with the fathers of our two friends as well: a couple of men of very differing ways of thought, yet whose opinions were in agreement in that they considered business the noblest occupation and in that they both paid the greatest attention to every advantage that any kind of speculation could bring to them. Old Meister had converted a valuable collection of pictures, drawings, etchings and antiques into money immediately after his father's death, had radically reconstructed and re-furnished his house according to the latest fashion and had made the rest of his means work for him in all possible ways. He had given a considerable portion of it to old Werner for him to utilize it, for the latter had a reputation as an energetic business-man whose speculations were usually favoured by fortune. But old Meister wanted nothing so much as to give his son qualities that he lacked himself and to bequeath to his children goods, on whose possession he laid the greatest value. Certainly he had a particular inclination to what was sumptuous and showy, but which at the same time should also have inner value and lastingness. Everything in his house had to be solid and massive, supplies to be plentiful, the silver heavy and the table-service costly; on the other hand the guests appeared rarely, for every meal became a festivity which could not be repeated frequently, both on account of the expense and of the discomfort. His household moved at a composed and uniform pace, and all the elements in it which were mobile and self-renewing were precisely those things that gave nobody much pleasure.

Old Werner led a completely different life in a dark and gloomy house. After finishing his day's work at the ancient desk in the cramped office, he liked to eat well and if possible drink even better, and what is more he did not care to enjoy good things on his own; apart from his family he always had to see at his table his friends and all strangers who had any connection at all with his house; his chairs were as old as the hills, but every day he invited someone to sit on them. The good food was what attracted the guests' attention, and nobody noticed that it was brought in on commonplace table-ware. His cellar did not hold much wine, but the wine that had been drunk at first was usually followed by a better one.

Thus the two fathers lived who often met and conferred about joint business enterprises, and on this very day were deciding on the dispatching of Wilhelm on a business journey.

'He can look around in the world,' old Meister was saying, 'and at the same time look after our business affairs in strange places; no greater favour can be shown to a young person than to introduce him in good time to his life's vocation. Your son returned so happily from his travels and was able to look after his business affairs so well that I am really curious to know how mine will get on; I'm afraid his experience will cost more than your son's.'

Old Meister, who had great ideas about his son and his son's abilities, said these words in the hope that his friend would contradict him and extol the young man's excellent gifts. But he was deceived in this; old Werner, who in practical matters never trusted anyone unless he had tested him himself, replied calmly: 'Everything must be tried; we can send him along the same route, we can give him directions for him to follow; there are various debts to be collected, old contacts to be taken up again, and new ones to be made. He can also help to promote the speculation which I was talking to you about recently; for there is not much that can be done unless precise data are collected on the spot.'

'Let him get ready,' said old Meister, 'and set off as soon as possible. Where shall we find him a horse that will be suitable for this expedition?'

'We shan't have far to look. A shopkeeper in H—, who owes us some money but otherwise is a good man, has offered me one in lieu of payment; my son has seen it, it is supposed to be quite a useful animal.'

'He can fetch it himself, and if he goes over there by mail-coach, he will be back in good time the day after tomorrow; in the meantime the portmanteau and letters can be got ready for him, and so he will be able to set out at the beginning of the coming week.'

Wilhelm was summoned and told about the decision. Who could be more delighted than he was when he found the means for his project put in his hands, the opportunity having been offered to him without his collaboration! So great was his enthusiasm, so pure was his conviction that he was acting fully aright in withdrawing from the oppressiveness of his life hitherto and following a new, nobler path, that his conscience was not disturbed in the slightest nor did any sense of worry arise in him, in fact he considered this deception rather as something sacred. He was sure that his parents and relations would in due course praise and bless him for taking this step, and he saw this concatenation of circumstances as the sign of a guiding fate.

How slowly time went for him until the hour when he should see his beloved again! He sat in his room and thought over his travel plans as an experienced thief or magician, when in imprisonment, occasionally draws his feet out of the firmly locked chains in order to encourage himself in the conviction that his liberation is possible, indeed that it is even closer than short-sighted warders believe.

At last the nightly hour struck; he left his house, shaking off all oppressiveness, and made his way through the quiet streets. At the big open square he raised his hands to the sky, and felt everything to be behind and below him; he had set himself free from everything. At one moment he fancied himself in the arms of his beloved, at another he was with her in the dazzling environment of the stage; he hovered in a profusion of hopes, and it was only now and again that the call of the nightwatchman reminded him that he was still walking upon this earth.

His beloved came to meet him on the steps, and how beautiful and lovely she was! She was wearing the new white négligé when she received him, and he believed that he had never yet seen her looking so attractive. In this way she was first using the gift of her absent admirer in the arms of her present one, and with true passion she lavished upon her darling the whole wealth of her caresses which nature suggested to her and which art had taught her; and is it necessary to ask her if she felt happy and blissful?

He revealed to her what had happened, and in general terms disclosed to her his plans and wishes. He told her that he would like to look for accommodation and then fetch her, and that he hoped she would not refuse him her hand in marriage. But the poor girl kept silent, concealed her tears and pressed her lover to her breast who, although he interpreted her silence in the most favourable way, none the less would have liked to have an answer, especially when he finally asked her in the most modest and friendly way whether he might not believe that he would be a father? But to this too she only replied with a sigh and a kiss.

Chapter Twelve

The next morning Mariane only awoke to fresh distress; she felt very much alone, did not want to see the day, stayed in bed and wept. The old woman sat beside her, tried to talk to her and console her; but she did not succeed in healing the wounded heart so quickly. Now the moment was near which the poor girl had been anticipating as if it were her last. Indeed, was it possible to feel as if one were in a more worrying situation? Her lover was departing, an irksome admirer was threatening to come, and the greatest disaster would be likely if, as was easily possible, the two should happen to meet.

'Calm yourself, love,' the old woman exclaimed; 'don't spoil your pretty eyes by crying! After all, is it such a great misfortune to have two lovers? And even if you can only give your caresses to the one, do at least be grateful to the other who, from the way in which he looks after you, certainly deserves to be called your friend.'

'My lover had a premonition that we would soon be separated', Mariane replied with tears; 'a dream revealed to him what we have been endeavouring so carefully to hide from him. He was sleeping so quietly at my side. All of a sudden I hear him stammering anxious, inaudible sounds. I get worried and wake him up. Oh, how lovingly and fondly and fierily he embraces me! "Oh Mariane!" he cried, "what a terrible condition it was that you saved me from! How am I to thank you for rescuing me from this hell? I dreamt that I was in an unknown area, and separated from you," he continued; "but your image hovered before me; I saw you on a beautiful hill, the sun was shining on the whole area; how attractive you seemed to me! But it was not long before I saw your image gliding down, always slipping down; I stretched out my arms to you, they did not reach across the distance. Your image went on sinking and came closer to a great lake which lay spread out wide at the foot of the hill, a swamp rather than a lake. All at once a man gave you his hand; he seemed to be trying to guide you upwards, but he was leading you sideways and appeared to be drawing you along behind himself. I called out, as I could not reach you, I hoped to warn you. When I tried to walk, the ground seemed to hold me firmly; when I could walk, the water hindered me, and even my cries were stifled in my anxious breast."—This was the poor man's story, as he recovered from his terror in my arms and considered himself happy to see a terrible dream supplanted by the most blissful reality.'

The old woman tried as well she could through her prosaic approach to attract her friend's poetry down to the level of ordinary life, and made use of the good device which bird-catchers usually employ successfully, when they take a little pipe and try to imitate the sounds of the creatures that they wish to see soon and frequently in their nets. She praised Wilhelm, speaking highly of his figure, his eyes and his love. The poor girl was glad to listen to her, got up, let herself be dressed and seemed quieter. 'My child, my darling,' the old woman continued in flattering tones, 'I don't want to upset you or offend you, I wouldn't think of stealing your happiness from you. Are you entitled to misinterpret my intentions, and have you forgotten that I have at all times cared more for you than for myself? Just tell me what it is you want; we will soon see how we can bring it about.'

'What can I want?' Mariane replied; 'I'm wretched, wretched to the core of my being; I love the man who loves me, see that I must part from him, and don't know how I can survive it. Norberg is coming, the man to whom we owe our whole existence, and whom we cannot do without. Wilhelm is very hemmed in, there's nothing he can do for me.'

'Yes, unfortunately he is one of those lovers who bring nothing but their hearts, and it is just this sort that have the greatest pretentions.'

'Don't make fun! The unhappy fellow is thinking of leaving his home to take up a theatre career and to offer me his hand in marriage.'

'We've already got four empty hands.'

'I've no choice,' Mariane continued, 'you decide! Push me in this direction or in that, only there's one thing you ought to know; it is likely that I am carrying within me a pledge that should bind us even more closely; think of this and decide; whom am I to leave, whom to follow?'

After a silence the old woman exclaimed: 'How youth always goes from one extreme to another! I find nothing more natural than to link everything together that brings us pleasure and advantage. If you love the one, let the other pay; it's only a matter of our being clever enough to keep them both apart from each other.'

'Do what you like, I can't think about anything at all; but I'll follow.'

'We have the advantage of being able to give as an excuse the peculiarity of the theatre-manager, who is proud of the morality of his troupe. Both lovers are already used to going about things in a secret and cautious manner. I'll take care of the time and the opportunity; only afterwards you must play the part which I prescribe for you. Who knows what circumstances may help us. If only Norberg would come now, when Wilhelm is away! Who is to stop you thinking of the one while in the arms of the other? I congratulate you on a son; may he have a wealthy father.'

Mariane was only cheered for a short time by these notions. She could not bring her circumstances into harmony with her emotions and convictions; she wanted to forget these painful conditions, and a thousand little details could not but remind her of them at every moment.

Chapter Thirteen

Meanwhile Wilhelm had ended his little journey and, not finding his business colleague at home, he handed over the letter of recommendation to the absent man's wife. But she gave him little information in answer to his questions; she was under great emotional strain, and the entire home was in great confusion.

It was not long, however, before she confided in him (and it could not be kept secret) that her stepdaughter had eloped with an actor, a man who a little while ago had severed his relationship with a company, had stayed in the locality and had given instruction in French. The father, beside himself with sorrow and annoyance, had rushed to the officials in order to have the fleeing pair pursued. She denigrated her daughter severely and disparaged the lover, so that no praiseworthy feature was left as far as the two of them were concerned, bemoaned at great length the shame which had been brought on the family by the matter, and put Wilhelm in no slight embarrassment, for he felt himself and his secret undertaking to be reprimanded and punished as it were in advance and with prophetic spirit by this Sibyl. But he could not help feeling an even stronger and more sincere sympathy with the sorrows of the father who came back from his office, telling the wife about his expedition with quiet sadness and half-completed phrases, and after reading the letter he had the horse brought forward for Wilhelm to see; he could not conceal his distraction and confusion.

Wilhelm thought that he would mount the horse straightaway and leave a household in which, the circumstances being what they were, it was impossible for him to feel at ease; but the good man did not want the departure to take place of the son of a house to which he owed so much without his being given hospitality and without having kept him for one night under his roof.

Our friend had taken a sad evening meal and put up with a disturbed night, and hastened in the early morning to take leave as soon as possible from people who, without knowing it, had tormented him most grievously with their stories and comments.

He was riding slowly and thoughtfully along the road when all at once he saw a number of armed men coming across the open country; from their long, wide coats with large lapels, their shapeless hats and clumsy weapons, their guileless walk and their easy-going demeanour, he immediately recognized them as a detachment of provincial militia. They halted under an old oak-tree, put down their muskets and settled comfortably on the grass in order to smoke their pipes. Wilhelm lingered with them and became involved in a conversation with a young man who came along on horseback. He had to listen once more unfortunately to the story of the two elopers, which was all too familiar to him, and what is more to hear comments which were not particularly favourable either to the young couple or to the parents. At the same time he learnt that they had come there to take charge really of the young couple, who had been overtaken and stopped in the nearby small town. Some time later a cart could be seen approaching from a distance; it was accompanied by a group of civic militia in a manner that was ridiculous rather than terrifying. An unwieldy-looking town-clerk rode at the head and exchanged greetings with the reciprocal actuarius (for this was the young man with whom Wilhelm had spoken) at the border with great conscientiousness and strange gestures, as may perhaps happen in the case of spirit and magician, where the one is inside the circle and the other outside it, in dangerous nocturnal operations.

Meanwhile the onlookers' attention had been caught by the farm cart, and they looked not without pity at the poor strays who were sitting side by side on a few bundles of straw gazing fondly at each other and hardly seeming to notice the bystanders. It had chanced to be necessary to transport them from the last village in such an unbecoming way because the old coach in which the beautiful woman was being carried had broken down. When this happened she asked if she might have the company of her friend who hitherto had had to walk alongside burdened with chains, since people had been convinced that he had been implicated in a capital crime. Indeed these chains contributed not a little to make the sight of the fond group more interesting, especially because the young man moved the chains with much charm when he repeatedly kissed his beloved's hands.

'We are very unfortunate,' she called to the people around; 'but not so guilty as we seem. This is the way cruel people reward true love, and parents, who neglect completely the happiness of their children, snatch them violently from the arms of the happiness which has come upon them after long, cheerless days!'

While the bystanders made their sympathy known in various

ways, the officials had completed their ceremonial; the cart moved on, and Wilhelm, who felt much concerned at the fate of the loving couple, hurried ahead on the footpath in order to make the acquaintance of the magistrate if possible before the procession arrived. But he had only just reached the magistrate's office, where everything was in commotion and ready to receive the elopers, when the actuarius caught him up and prevented any other conversation by giving an elaborate account of the way everything had gone, in particular by long-winded praise of his horse, which he had only bought the day previously from a Jew.

The unfortunate couple had already been deposited by the garden which was linked with the magistrate's office by a little door, and they had been led in quietly. The actuarius accepted from Wilhelm the latter's sincere praise at this considerate treatment, although really he only did this in order to tease the crowd that had gathered in front of the office and to deprive them of the agreeable spectacle of the humiliation of a lady who was their fellow-citizen.

The magistrate, who was no special lover of such extraordinary cases, because he mostly made some mistake or another over them and in return for the best of intentions was usually rewarded by the princely government with a sharp reproof, walked with heavy steps to the office where he was followed by the actuarius, Wilhelm and some respected citizens.

Firstly the beautiful woman was led forward, and she entered without impertinence, calmly and self-confidently. The way she was dressed and the way she behaved in general showed that she was a girl who took some pride in herself. Without being asked, she also started to talk about her circumstances in a not improper manner.

The actuarius ordered her to be silent and held his pen over the piece of paper that he had started writing on. The magistrate composed himself, looked at him, cleared his throat, and asked the poor child what her name was and how old she might be.

'I beg of you, sir,' she replied, 'it is bound to seem strange to me that you should ask me my name and age, as you know very well what I am called, and that I am as old as your eldest son. I shall be glad to tell you without further ado what you wish to know of me and what you have to know.

'Since my father's second marriage I have not been having the best of treatment at home. I could have made several good matches, if my stepmother had not succeeded in thwarting them because of her fear of the cost of a dowry. Then I met young Melina and could not but fall in love with him, and as we anticipated the obstacles standing in the way of our union, we resolved to seek together in the wide world a happiness that did not seem to be granted to us at home. I took nothing with me that was not my own; we did not make off as thieves and robbers, and my lover does not deserve to be dragged around weighed down with chains and bonds. The prince is just, he will not tolerate this severity. If we are punishable, then not in this way.'

The old magistrate experienced a double, indeed threefold, sense of embarrassment at this. He could already hear reprimands from the highest level buzzing around his head, and the girl's fluent speech had completely upset his planning of protocol. Things became even more troublesome when she would not go into the question further after orderly questions had been repeatedly put to her, but firmly referred to what she had just said.

'I am not a criminal,' she said. 'I have been brought here in shame on bundles of straw; there is a higher justice which should honorably reinstate us.'

In the meantime the actuarius had been writing down what she said, and he whispered to the magistrate that he should just carry on; a formal protocol could be drawn up afterwards.

The old man plucked up courage again and now began to inquire in arid words and traditional dry formulae about the sweet secrets of love.

Wilhelm's face reddened, and the cheeks of the sweet miscreant were likewise enlivened by the charming colour of modesty. She was silent and hesitated, until at last embarrassment itself seemed to heighten her courage.

'Let me assure you,' she exclaimed, 'that I would be strong enough to confess the truth, even if I had to speak against myself; ought I to falter and stop now that it does me credit? Yes, from the moment that I was sure of his affection and fidelity, I have regarded him as my husband; I have gladly conceded to him everything that love demands and which a heart that is sure cannot deny. Now do with me what you like. If I was reluctant to confess for a moment, the only reason for this was the fear that my admission might have bad consequences for my lover.'

When he heard her confession, Wilhelm formed a high opinion of the girl's way of thinking, even though the judiciary saw her as an impudent wanton and the citizens present thanked God that such cases had not occurred in their families or else had not become known.

At this moment Wilhelm placed his Mariane before the tribunal, placed even finer phrases on her lips, caused her honesty to become even more sincere and her confession even nobler. He was overcome by the most intensely passionate wish to help the two lovers. He did not conceal it and covertly asked the hesitating magistrate to bring the affair to a conclusion, saying that everything was as clear as it could be and did not need any further investigation.

This helped so much that the girl was asked to withdraw, but in her place the young man was summoned, after the fetters had been removed from him outside the door. He seemed to take a more thoughtful view of his fate. His replies were steadier, and if from one point of view he showed less heroic frankness, on the other hand he recommended himself by the definite and orderly quality of his statement.

After the conclusion of this hearing which tallied in every respect with the previous one, except that he obstinately denied, in order to spare the girl, what she had already admitted, she too was told to appear again, and there took place between the two of them a scene which completely won over our friend's heart to their cause.

He saw here before his eyes in an unpleasant court room something that usually only happens in novels and plays: the conflict of mutual generosity of spirit, and the strength of love in misfortune.

'For is it therefore true,' he said to himself, 'that a shy fondness which hides itself from the eye of the sun and the eyes of men and only ventures to find enjoyment in secluded solitude and deep secrecy, can show itself as braver, stronger and bolder than other passions which are effervescent and boasting, when it is brought into the open through an inimical mischance?'

To his relief the whole procedure terminated fairly soon. They were both taken into a tolerable form of custody, and if it had been possible, he would have taken the young lady to her parents that very evening. For he had firmly made up his mind to act as mediator here and to promote the happy and respectable union of the two lovers.

He asked the magistrate for permission to speak with Melina on his own, and this was then granted to him without difficulty.

Chapter Fourteen

The conversation of the two new acquaintances quite soon became intimate and lively. For when Wilhelm disclosed to the downcast youth his connection with the young lady's parents, offered himself as mediator, and himself showed keen hopes, the sad and worried spirit of the prisoner cheered up, he felt as if he were liberated already and reconciled with his parents-in-law, and it was now a question of his future livelihood and accommodation.

'You surely won't be in a predicament about that,' said Wilhelm; 'for both of you seem to be destined by nature to make your fortune in the profession which you have chosen. An agreeable figure, a pleasant sounding voice, a heart full of feeling! Can actors be better endowed? If I can help you with some recommendations, I shall be very pleased.'

'I am deeply grateful to you,' rejoined the other; 'but I shall probably hardly be able to make use of them, for I'm not thinking of going back to the theatre, if possible.'

'It is very wrong of you to think like that,' Wilhelm said after a pause in which he had recovered from his astonishment; for he had been convinced that the actor would make for the theatre as soon as he had been set free with his young wife. This seemed as natural and necessary to him as it would be for a frog to seek water. He had not doubted it for a moment, and now to his surprise he had to learn of the opposite intention.

'Yes,' added the other, 'I have made up my mind not to return to the theatre, but rather to take up some form of civic work, I don't mind what it is so long as I can get a post.'

'That is a strange decision, which I can't approve of; for unless there's a special reason, it is never advisable to change the way of life which one has taken up, and in any case I don't know of any profession which could offer so many attractions and alluring prospects as that of the actor.'

'It's obvious that you've never been one,' the former replied.

Wilhelm said in answer to this: 'Sir, how rarely is man contented with the condition in which he finds himself! He always covets that of his neighbour, and the latter likewise yearns to be out of his own condition.'

'Yet there is a difference,' Melina rejoined, 'between what is bad and what is worse; it is experience, not impatience, that makes me act like this. Is any way on earth of earning a scrap of bread less certain and more difficult than this one? It would be almost as good to go begging from door to door. What we have to put up with from the envy of colleagues, the bias of the manager, and the fickle moods of the public! In truth, you have to have a skin as thick as that of a bear that is led around on a chain in the company of monkeys and dogs and beaten so that it will dance at the sound of bagpipes before children and the rabble.'

Wilhelm had all sorts of thoughts in this context, but he did not want to say them direct to this good man's face. So in this conversation he skirted round the topic at a distance. The other expressed himself all the more openly and expansively.

'Isn't it necessary,' he said, 'for a theatre manager to go on hands and knees to every alderman, just to get permission to cause a little more money to circulate in a place for four weeks while the fair is on? I've often been sorry for our manager, who was a good man in a number of ways, though at other times he gave me cause for discontent. A good actor enhances him, he can't get rid of the bad ones; and if he tries to equate to some extent his income and his expenditure, this is at once too much for the public, the theatre stands empty, and in order not to collapse altogether, the show has to go on with losses and worry. No sir! Since you feel inclined to take up our cause, as you say, I beg you to speak in the most serious manner with the parents of my beloved! If I am provided for here, given a little job as clerk or collector, I shall consider myself lucky.'

After they had conversed a little further, Wilhelm left, promising to approach the parents quite early next morning and to see what he could do. No sooner was he on his own than he had to ventilate his feelings in the following exclamations: 'Unhappy Melina, it is not in your profession but in yourself that the paltry element lies, over which you cannot be master! Would not anybody in the world who took up a handicraft, an art or any way of life without an inner vocation be compelled, as you are, to find his position intolerable? Whoever is born *with* a talent, *to* a talent, finds here his finest form of existence! Nothing on earth is without troublesomeness! It is only the inner drive, liking and love that help us overcome obstacles, prepare paths and raise ourselves above the narrow circle within which others wear themselves out with anxiety. For you the boards of the stage are only boards, and the parts are like homework to a schoolboy. You see the audience in the way they appear to themselves on workdays. So it could certainly be all the same to you to be sitting over ruled books at a desk, entering up interest and poking out remainders. You do not feel the conflagrating, concurrent whole, which is invented, comprehended and executed by the spirit alone; you do not feel that there is in human beings a brighter spark which, unless it is nurtured and fanned, will be more deeply covered by the ashes of daily needs and indifference, and yet will be stifled so late, indeed almost never. You feel in your soul no strength to blow upon this spark, in your own heart no riches so that nourishment may be given to what has been aroused. It is hunger that drives you on, discomforts are repulsive to you, and it is hidden from you that these enemies lurk in every profession and that they can only be overcome with cheerfulness and equanimity. You do well to long to be within those limits imposed by a commonplace job; for what work would you be able to accomplish which requires spirit and courage? Air your views to a soldier, a statesman or a priest, and with just as much right he will be able to complain about the wretched aspects of his profession. Indeed, have there not been people who were so bereft of all vital feeling that they have declared the whole life and nature of mortal men to be a nothing, an existence that is miserable and like dust? If the figures of active personalities stirred in living form within your soul, if ardent sympathy warmed your heart, if the mood that comes from the deepest recesses within diffused your whole being, if the sounds from your throat and the words of your lips were attractive to hear, if you felt sufficient within yourself, you would certainly seek out the place and opportunity to be able to feel yourself in others.'

In the course of such words and such thoughts our friend had undressed and got into bed with a feeling of most intense satisfaction. A whole novel developed in his imagination with regard to what he could do next day in the place of the unworthy man, pleasant fantasies accompanied him gently into the realm of sleep and left him there to their sisters, the dreams which enveloped him with open arms and surrounded our friend's head with the model of heaven.

Early next morning he was already awake again and was thinking over his forthcoming negotiations. He went back to the house of the deserted parents where he was received with surprise. He presented his concern in modest terms and found quite soon both more and fewer difficulties than he had assumed. Things had happened now, and although extremely severe and hard people are accustomed to setting themselves violently against what is past and cannot be altered, on the other hand what has already happened has an irresistible force in its action upon the feelings of most people, and what appeared impossible takes it place alongside the everyday as soon as it has actually happened. It was therefore soon agreed that Mr. Melina should marry the daughter; however, because of her bad behaviour she was not to take any marriage portion and was to promise to leave an aunt's legacy in her father's hands for some years longer, in return for small interest. The second point, that of some civic employment, led to considerably greater difficulties. The parents did not want to see the undutiful child, they did not want to be constantly reminded by the presence of the young couple that this was the union of a nobody with such a reputable family, one that was even related to a senior church minister; there was just as little hope that the princely councils would entrust him with a post. Both parents were equally strong against it, and Wilhelm could achieve nothing with all his arguments, although he spoke very ardently in favour, because he had a poor opinion of the man and did not want him to return to the theatre, being convinced that he did not merit such good fortune. If he had been aware of the hidden motivations, he would not have given himself the trouble at all of endeavouring to persuade the parents. For the father, who would have been glad to keep the daughter at home, hated the young man, because his wife herself had taken a fancy to him, and she could not tolerate the presence of her stepdaughter as a happy rival to herself. And so, against his will, Melina had to set off after a few days with his young bride, who for her part showed a greater keenness to see the world and to let herself be seen by it, in order that they might find employment with some theatre company or other.

Chapter Fifteen

Happy period of youth! Happy times of the first desire for love! Man is then like a child amusing itself for hours on end with an echo, carrying the weight of the conversation by itself, and well satisfied with the entertainment, even if the invisible interlocutor only repeats the last syllables of the words that have been called out.

Wilhelm was like this in the earlier times of his passion for Mariane, but particularly in the later times too, when he transferred the whole wealth of his feeling to her and in so doing saw himself as a beggar living from her alms. And just as a tract of country seems more attractive, indeed only attractive, to us when it is lit by the sun, so everything that surrounded and had contact with her was in his eyes made more beautiful and more splendid.

How often he stood behind the scenes in the theatre, having been given the manager's permission as a privilege! It was true that the magic of perspective was then lost, but the much more potent enchantment of love could now start to have its effect. He could stand for hours by the dirty light-carrier, breathing in the fumes of the tallow lamps, looking out for his beloved, and when she appeared again and looked at him in a friendly way, be lost in rapture and, when close to the structure of joists and boards, feel as if transported into a paradisaic state. The stuffed lambs, the taffeta waterfalls, the pasteboard rose bushes and the one-sided straw huts evoked in him fond poetic visions of an ancient pastoral world. Even the dancers, who looked ugly at close quarters, were not always repulsive to him, because they were appearing on *one* stage with his much beloved one. And so it is certain that love, which must first give life to arbours of roses, woods of myrtles and moonlight, can also give a semblance of living nature even to shavings of wood and scraps of paper. Love is such a strong seasoning that even insipid and disagreeable broths become tasty because of it.

Indeed such a seasoning was necessary to make that condition tolerable, in fact subsequently agreeable, in which he usually found her room, indeed occasionally her herself.

Having been brought up in an elegant patrician house, Wilhelm knew order and cleanliness as the element in which he breathed, and as he had inherited something of his father's love of ostentation, he would as a boy deck out in a stately manner his room, which he regarded as his own little kingdom. His bed-curtains were gathered up into great folds and fastened with tassels, in a way comparable to that in which one imagines thrones to be; he had been able to have a carpet for the centre of the room and a finer covering for the table; he placed his books and utensils almost automatically in such a way that a Dutch painter would have been able to select good groups for his still lives. He had arranged a white cap like a turban and had had the sleeves of his dressing-gown cut short in the manner of an oriental costume. But he gave the reason for this as being that the long, wide sleeves hindered him while writing. When he was quite on his own in the evening and no longer needed to fear that he might be disturbed, he usually wore a silk sash round his body, and he is said often to have stuck into this girdle a dagger which he had appropriated from an old armoury, and in this way to have memorized and rehearsed the tragic roles allocated to him, indeed in this guise too he is said to have kneeled on the carpet to pray.

How happy, therefore, he had considered in earlier times actors whom he saw as possessing so many majestic garments, armour and weapons and as being in the constant exercise of noble deportment, whose spirit seemed to mirror the most magnificent and pleasant elements in circumstances, opinions and passions that the world had brought forth. Likewise Wilhelm also assumed that the domestic life of an actor was a sequence of dignified actions and occupations, of which appearing on the stage was the topmost peak, rather as silver, having been a long time in the purifying fire, at last appears in colourful beauty before the eyes of the worker and at the same time indicates to him that the metal has now been cleansed of all alien alloys.

How startled he, therefore, was at first when he was at his beloved's and could look beyond the happy haze surrounding him to tables, chairs and floor. Like the gleaming attire of a fish that has lost its scales, the wreckage of light, momentary and deceptive finery lay scattered about in wild disorder. The implements of personal hygiene, such as combs, soap and cloths, with the traces of their use, were similarly not concealed. Music, acting-parts and shoes, linen and Italian flowers, cases, hairpins, make-up pots and ribbons, books and straw-hats, none of these despised the propinquity of the other, all were united by a common factor, by powder and dust. However, as in her presence Wilhelm noticed little of anything else, rather indeed as everything that belonged to her or had touched her could not but become dear to him, in the end he discovered in this confused way a charm which he had never felt in his stately, ostentatious orderliness. He felt—if now he took away her corsets in order to get to the piano, now placed her skirts on the bed, in order to be able to sit down, if she herself in unconstrained openness did not attempt to hide from him many a natural action which people usually conceal from others out of a sense of seemliness—he felt, I say, as if he were coming closer to her with every moment, as if a link between them was being established by invisible ties.

It was not so easy for him to reconcile the behaviour of the other actors, whom he often encountered in her company during his first visits, with his own ideas. Bustling about and yet idle, the last thing they seemed to think about was their profession and purpose; he never heard them speak about the poetic value of a play nor pass judgment, either rightly or wrongly, on it; the only questions were always: "What will the play make? Will it be a draw? How long a run will it have? How often can it be put on?" and further questions and comments of this kind. Then they habitually pulled the manager to pieces, because he was too mean with payment, and was unjust to this one or that; then they went for the audience, because its applause seldom rewarded the right man, because the place of the German theatre was improving daily, actors were being honoured ever more according to their deserts and could not be honoured too much. Then there was a lot of talk about coffee-houses and vineyards and what had happened there, how many debts some colleague owed and the deductions he would have to suffer, the disproportions in the weekly wages and the intrigues of a counter-group; for in the end after all the great and merited attention of the public was considered again, and the influence of the theatre on the cultural development of a nation and of the world was not forgotten.

All these things, which had already on earlier occasions caused Wilhelm many an unquiet hour, filled his mind again as his horse carried him slowly home and he considered the various incidents that had befallen him. He had seen with his own eyes the disturbing effect of the flight of a girl on a good middle-class family, indeed on a whole little town; the scenes on the country road and in the magistrate's office, Melina's opinions, and other things that had happened, haunted him again and brought to his lively, eager mind a kind of anxious restlessness with which he could not put up for long; he spurred on his horse and hastened towards the town.

Yet in following this course too he only involved himself in new unpleasantness. Werner, his friend and presumptive brother-in-law, was waiting for him in order to engage in a serious, significant and unexpected conversation with him.

Werner was one of those tried people who are fixed in their way of life and who are usually referred to as cold because on provocation they do not flare up quickly or visibly; what is more, his contact with Wilhelm was a continuous altercation, though this actually only linked them with one another more firmly: for notwithstanding their differing ways of thought each reaped advantage from the other. Werner rather prided himself on the fact that he could occasionally bridle and curb Wilhelm's fine, though sometimes excessive imagination, and Wilhelm often had a sense of magnificent triumph if he carried his circumspect friend along with him in an outburst of emotion. Thus the one tested himself against the other, they grew accustomed to seeing each other every day, and it could be said that the impulse to find one another and to discuss together was increased by the impossibility of their being understandable to one another. Basically, however, as they were both good people, they went side by side together with one aim in view and could never understand why neither of them could bring round the other to his point of view.

For some time Werner had noticed that Wilhelm's visits were becoming less frequent, that he would break off abruptly and distractedly while discussing favourite themes, and that he no longer became absorbed in the ardent developing of strange ideas, for it is here indeed that an open spirit, which finds quiet and satisfaction in the presence of a friend, can be truly recognized. The precise and circumspect Werner at first looked for the failing in his own behaviour until some town talk led him on to the right track and some incautious remarks of Wilhelm brought him nearer to certainty. He began investigating and learnt quite soon that Wilhelm had been openly visiting an actress for some time, had been talking with her in the theatre and taking her home; he would have been inconsolable, if he had also known about the nightly meetings; for what he heard was that Mariane was a seductive young woman who would probably do his friend out of money and what is more would let herself be kept at the same time by a most unworthy lover.

As soon as he had converted his suspicion as far as was possible to certainty, he decided to launch an attack on Wilhelm, and was fully prepared in all respects when the latter was just coming back from his journey, annoyed and upset.

On the same evening Werner recounted everything he knew to him, calmly at first, and then with the urgent seriousness of a well-meaning friend, leaving no aspect unclear and letting his friend taste all the bitterness that quiet people with their virtuous gloating are accustomed to distributing so lavishly to those in love. But as can be imagined, he did not accomplish very much. Wilhelm replied with inward emotion, but with great certainty; 'You don't know the girl! Appearances are not perhaps in her favour, but I am as sure of her fidelity and virtue as I am of my own love.'

Werner insisted upon his accusation and offered proofs and witnesses. Wilhelm rejected them and left his friend in an irritated and shocked state of mind, like someone whose defective but firmly fixed tooth has been held and vainly wrenched at by a clumsy dentist.

It was highly disturbing for Wilhelm to see the beautiful picture of Mariane in his mind's eye clouded and almost disfigured, firstly by the vagaries of the journey, and then by Werner's unfriendliness. He made use of the surest way of restoring for himself full clarity and beauty by hastening to her by night along the usual ways. She received him with lively joy; for he had ridden past on arrival, she had expected him that night, and it can be imagined that all misgivings were soon banished from his heart. Indeed, her tenderness re-awakened his complete confidence, and he told her how greatly she had been wronged by public talk and by his friend.

They had many a lively conversation about the first period of their acquaintanceship, the memory of which remains as one of the most agreeable entertainments of two lovers. The first steps that take us into the maze of love are so pleasant, and the prospects so attractive, that we like to recall them only too willingly. Each partner tries to retain an advantage over the other: the one may claim to have loved sooner, more selflessly, and each wishes to be defeated rather than to be victorious in this contest.

Wilhelm repeated to Mariane what she had heard so often before, that she had soon deflected his attention from the play to herself alone, that her figure, her acting, her voice had enthralled him; how finally he had only gone to see those plays in which she had a part, how at last he had crept behind the scenes and had often stood close to her without being noticed by her; then he spoke delightedly of the happy evening on which he had found an opportunity to do her a favour and to embark on a conversation.

Mariane on the other hand did not want to concede that she had not noticed him for so long; she maintained that she had seen him walking, and as proof described to him the clothing he had been wearing on that particular day; she maintained that she had found him more pleasing than all others at that time, and that she had wished to make his acquaintance.

How gladly Wilhelm believed all this! How gladly he let himself be persuaded that she had been drawn to him by an irresistible attraction when he had approached her, that she had stepped beside him in the wings intentionally, in order to see him at closer quarters and to become acquainted with him, and that in the end, as his reserve and bashfulness could not be overcome, she had given him an opportunity herself and had so to speak pressed him to go and fetch her a glass of lemonade.

In the course of this loving contest, which they pursued through all the little episodes of their brief romance, the hours passed very quickly for them, and Wilhelm left his beloved fully reassured and firmly intending to put his plan into immediate operation.

Chapter Sixteen

His father and mother had looked after what he needed for his departure; it was only a few details missing in the equipment that delayed his setting-off for some days. Wilhelm made use of this time in order to write a letter to Mariane in which he wanted at last to refer to the matter which up to now she had always avoided talking to him about. This is how the letter ran:

'Beneath the dear cover of night, which at other times enveloped me when I was in your arms, I am sitting and thinking and writing to you, and what I think of and get on with is only for your sake. Oh, Mariane! I, the happiest of men, feel like a bridegroom who intuitively anticipates what new world will develop in and through him as he stands on the festive carpets and in the course of the holy ceremony places himself, in thoughts full of desire, before the mysterious curtains from whence the fondness of love whispers towards him.

'I have persuaded myself not to see you for some days; this was easy, bearing in mind the hope of the recompense of being with you and being your own for ever! Am I to repeat what I would like? And yet it is necessary; for it seems as if you have not understood me up to now.

'How often have I searched in your heart for an indication of a request for an eternal union; this I have done in gentle tones of a fidelity which dares to say little because it hopes to fulfil all. You will have understood me certainly, for the wish must be budding in your heart; you will have heard me in every kiss and in the nestling quiet of those happy evenings. It was then that I came to know your modesty, and how my love was increased! Where another would have behaved affectedly in order by means of unnecessary sunlight to ripen a decision in the heart of her lover, to entice forth a declaration and to confirm a promise, in this respect you hold back, you close once more the heart of your beloved when it is half-open for confidences, and through an apparent indifference you try to hide your agreement; but I do understand you! What a wretched fellow I should be if I did not recognize in these signs a pure, unselfish love which is solicitous only for your friend! Do trust me and be calm! We belong to each other, and neither of us will leave or lose the other, if we live for each other.

'Accept this hand! Solemnly this further, superfluous token is offered! We have felt all the joys of love, but there is new bliss in the confirmation of the concept of permanence. Do not ask: how? Have no fear! Fate makes provision for love, and all the more certainly since love is unassuming.

'My heart left my parents' house a long time ago; it is with you, just as my spirit haunts the stage. O my beloved! Has indeed anyone been granted to such an extent as myself the possibility of combining his aspirations? No sleep comes over my eyes, and your love and happiness rise before me like an eternal dawn of the day.

'It is difficult for me to restrain myself, and not spring up and run to you and force you to give your consent and set out straightaway in the morning to press on further into the world in search of my aim.—No, I will hold myself back! I will not thoughtlessly take foolish, audacious steps; my plan has been sketched, and I wish to carry it out quietly.

'I know the theatre-manager Serlo, my journey will go straight to him, on a number of occasions a year ago he wished that his people had something of my liveliness and enthusiasm for the theatre, and I shall certainly be welcomed by him; for I would rather not become a member of your company for several reasons; what is more, Serlo's theatre is so far from here that I shall be able to cover my tracks at first. I shall be able to make a tolerable living there without delay; I shall take a look round the theatre-public, get to know the company and send for you later.

'Mariane, you see what I can bring myself to do, in order to make sure of you; for I can't truly allow myself to think that I may not see you for such a long time, knowing that you are about in the wide world! But then if I imagine again your love which secures me against everything, if you do not reject my proposal before we part, and if you give me your hand in the presence of the priest, I shall go quietly. It is only a formula between us, but such a beautiful formula, the blessing of heaven added to the blessing of earth. It can be arranged easily and secretly in the neighbourhood, on knightly territory.

'I've money enough for the start; if we share what we have, it will be enough for both of us; before this amount has been spent, heaven will provide further.

'Yes, darling, I'm not at all anxious. What is begun with so much cheerfulness must come to a happy end. I have never doubted that someone who is serious about it can get on in the world, and I feel that I have courage enough to be able to make a reasonable living for two, indeed several. "The world is thankless," many say; I haven't yet found that it is thankless, provided you know how to do something for it in the right way. My entire soul glows at the thought of making my appearance at last and speaking to men's hearts about what they have been yearning to hear for so long. How many times have I, who am so fascinated by the theatre's magnificence, felt fearful when I have seen the most wretched people flatter themselves that they can move our hearts with great and apposite words! A falsetto note sounds much better and purer; it is unbelievable the way these fellows go wrong in their crude clumsiness.

'The theatre has often been in conflict with the pulpit; they ought not to squabble with one another, it seems to me. How very desirable it would be if in both places God and nature were glorified only by noble-minded people! These are no dreams, my dearest! Just as I have been able to feel from your heart that you are in love, so also I seize the dazzling thought and say—I won't say it out loud, but I shall hope that at some future date we shall appear as a pair of good spirits to people, to open their hearts, to touch their emotions and to prepare heavenly delights for them, as surely as joys have been granted to me at your breast which must always be called heavenly, because in those moments we feel transported and elated beyond ourselves.

'I don't know how to close; I have already said too much, and do not know whether I have already told you everything, everything that is of concern to you; for the movement of the wheel that turns in my heart cannot be expressed in words.

'Meanwhile receive this note, my love! I have read it through again and find that I ought to start all over again; but it contains everything that you need to know which is a preparation for you for the time when I shall soon return to your bosom with the gaiety of sweet love. I appear to myself like a prisoner who is filing at his fetters, listening in a dungeon. I will say good-night to my parents in their carefree sleep!—Goodbye, beloved! Goodbye! I am closing, for now; my eyes have closed two or three times; it is already deep in the night.'

Chapter Seventeen

The day would not come to an end as Wilhelm, with his letter folded neatly in his pocket, longed to be with Mariane; furthermore, it had scarcely started to grow dark when he crept off to her quarters against his custom. His plan was to indicate that he would be coming for the night, to leave his beloved again for a short time, to press the letter in her hand before he went away, and on his return later in the night to receive her answer and consent, or to compel these through the power of his caresses. He flew into her arms and could scarcely become composed again in her embrace. The strength of his feelings concealed from him at first that she was not responding with cordiality as she usually did; however, she could not conceal her troubled state for long; she gave illness, indisposition as a pretext; she complained of headache, she did not want to take up the suggestion that he would like to come back that night. He did not suspect anything wrong, did not press her further, but felt that it was not the right time to give her his letter. He kept it, and as various of her movements and utterances were urging him politely to go away, in the passion of his avid love he seized one of her scarves and put it in his pocket, and reluctantly took leave of her lips and turned from her door. He crept home, but was unable to stay there long either, put on different clothes and once more sought the fresh air.

When he had gone up and down a few streets he encountered a stranger who asked the way to a particular inn; Wilhelm offered to show him where it was; the stranger inquired about the name of the street, about the owners of various large buildings which they passed, and then about some of the town's police regulations, and they were involved in quite an interesting conversation when they arrived at the inn door. The stranger pressed his guide to enter and drink a glass of punch with him; at the same time he informed him of his name and his birthplace, and also of the business that had brought him here, and asked Wilhelm for similar confidences. The latter did not hesitate to give his name and also his address.

'Aren't you a grandson of the old Meister who owned the beautiful art collection?' the stranger asked.

'Yes, I am. I was ten years old when Grandfather died, and it grieved me very much to see those beautiful things sold.'

'Your father obtained a large sum of money for them.'

'You know about it, then?'

'Oh yes, I saw those treasures when they were still in your house. Your grandfather was not merely a collector, he knew something about art, he had been to Italy in an earlier, happy time, and had brought back from there treasures which couldn't be had now at any price. He owned fine pictures by the best masters; one scarcely trusted one's eyes when one looked through his sketches; there were some priceless fragments among the marble pieces he possessed; he owned a very instructive sequence of bronzes; similarly he had collected his coins relating to art and history in a purposeful manner; the few cut stones he had merited every praise; furthermore, the whole collection was well presented, even though the rooms and halls of the old house were not symmetrically constructed.'

'You can think what we children lost, when all the things were taken down and packed away. These were the first sad times of my life. I still remember how empty the rooms appeared to us, when we saw the gradual disappearance of objects which had entertained us from childhood onwards and which we took to be as unchangeable as the house and the town themselves.'

'Unless I'm mistaken, your father invested the capital he had obtained in the enterprise of a neighbour with whom he entered into a kind of business association?'

'Quite right! And their speculations made in partnership have turned out very well for them; in the last twelve years their means have increased a lot, and both of them are consequently only the more enthusiastic about business; also old Werner has a son who is much more suited to this type of work than I am.'

'I am sorry that this locality has lost so great an attraction as your grandfather's collection used to be. I saw it shortly before it was sold, and I may venture to say that I was the reason for the sale having materialized. A rich nobleman, a man of great taste and enthusiasm, who, however, in the case of such an important transaction did not wish to rely entirely on his own judgment, had sent me here and asked for my advice. I examined the collection for six days, and on the seventh I advised my friend to pay the whole sum that was asked for without hesitation. You, as a lively boy, were often around me; you explained the subjects of the paintings to me and generally knew how to interpret the collection really well.'

'I do remember such a person, but I should never have recognized you as he.'

'It is quite a time ago too, and we do change, either more or less. If I remember aright, you had a favourite picture among the paintings, and you did not want to let me get away from it.'

'Quite right! It portrayed the story of how the sick prince consumes himself in love for his father's bride-to-be.'[1]

'It wasn't in fact the best of the paintings, not well composed, of no particular colouring, and the execution was completely mannered.'

'I didn't understand that, and still don't understand it; it is the subject-matter that attracts me about a painting, not the art.'

'Your grandfather seemed to think differently in this connection; for the greatest part of his collection consisted of excellent things where the merit of the painter could always be admired, whatever themes the paintings might offer; what is more, this particular picture hung in the outermost ante-room, as a sign that he thought less of it.'

'It was just there that we were always allowed to play as children and that this picture made upon me an indelible impression which even your criticism, which incidentally I respect,

1. A painting in Kassel art gallery, now ascribed to Antonio Belucci (1654-1726), has been suggested as providing Goethe with this motif. (Tr.)

would not be able to eradicate, even if we were standing in front of the picture now. How sorry I felt, and still do feel, for a youth who has to lock up within himself the sweet urges, the most beautiful heritage that nature gave us, and conceal within his heart the fire which was intended to warm and enliven himself and others, so that his innermost being is consumed in monstrous pains! How unhappy I feel for the unhappy woman who is expected to devote herself to someone else when her heart has already found the worthy object of a true and pure desire!'

'These feelings are certainly very far removed from those considerations which influence an art critic when he looks at the works of great masters; but presumably, if the collection had remained the property of your family, you would have gradually developed an appreciation of the meaning of the works themselves, so that you would not always have seen only yourself and your own inclinations in works of art.'

'Certainly, the sale of the collection was something I very much regretted straightaway, and indeed I have often missed it in more mature years as well; but when I consider that it was, so to speak, destined to be thus so that a fancy and a talent could be developed in me which were to have much more effect on my life than those inanimate pictures, I am glad to acquiesce and to revere the fate which is to devise what is best for me and what is best for everybody.'

'I am sorry to hear once more the word fate being spoken by a young man who is just at the age when it is usual to subordinate the aims of higher beings to man's vivid inclinations.'

'So you don't believe in any destiny? In any power that holds sway over us and guides everything for the best for us?'

'It is not a matter of my faith now, nor is this the place to analyse how I try to make the things which are incomprehensible to all of us appear to some extent capable of being conceived by myself; here the only question is which way of imagining is most advantageous to us. The texture of this world is made up out of necessity and chance; man's higher reason comes between the two and can dominate them; it can guide, lead and make use of chance factors, and only when it stands firm and unshakeable, does man deserve to be called a god of the earth. Unhappy is he who from early years becomes accustomed to trying to find something arbitrary in what is necessary, who would like to attribute to chance elements a kind of higher reason, the following of which would in fact be a matter of religion. Does that mean anything more than to renounce one's inclinations? We delude ourselves that we are pious by sauntering along without reflection, letting ourselves be determined by pleasant chance factors, and finally giving the result of such a precarious life the name of divine guidance.'

'Did it never happen to you that a small circumstance caused you to follow a certain path, on which an agreeable opportunity soon offered itself, and a series of unexpected events finally brought you to the goal which you yourself had as yet scarcely envisaged? Should not this instil resignation to fate and confidence in such guidance?'

'With those opinions no maiden could keep her virtue, and nobody could keep his money in his purse; for there are inducements enough to get rid of both. I can only be happy about the man who knows what is useful to him and to others and labours to limit the element of caprice in his life. Everyone has his fortune in his hands, just as the artist has the raw material which he wishes to re-shape into a figure. But with this art it is the same as with all; only the capacity for it is innate, the art has to be learnt and carefully practised.'

This and other topics were discussed between them for some time longer; finally they separated, without their appearing to have convinced each other particularly, but they did arrange a place where they should meet on the next day.

Wilhelm went up and down several streets; he could hear clarinets, French horns and bassoons, and his heart responded. Itinerant minstrels were playing pleasant serenade music. He spoke to them, and in return for some money they followed him to Mariane's quarters. Tall trees adorned the square in front of her house, and he posted his singers among them; he himself reposed on a seat some distance away and yielded wholly to the floating sounds which murmured around him in the comforting night air. Stretched out beneath the gracious stars, he felt his existence to be a golden dream.—'These flutes she can hear too,' he said to himself inwardly; 'she will feel whose remembrance and whose love is making the night harmonious; at some distance too we are bound together by these melodies, just as at any distance we are held by the most delicate mood of love. Oh, two loving hearts are like two magnetic clocks; whatever moves in the one must move the other as well; for there is only *one* factor that functions in both, *one* force that permeates them. Can I, when in her arms, sense any possibility of being separated from her? And yet I shall be far from her, shall seek a safe place for our love and shall always have it with me.

'How often has it happened to me that, when separated from her and lost in thoughts of her, I touched a book or a dress, or something else, and believed that I could feel her hand, so completely was I surrounded by her presence. And to remember those moments which shun the light of day just as the eye of the cold observer and for whose enjoyment gods might well decide to leave the painless condition of pure blessedness!—Remember?—As if one could renew in memory the transport of the intoxicating cup which deprives our senses, enmeshed in heavenly bonds, of their whole composure—And her figure—.' He lost himself in thinking about her, his calmness turned into desire, he embraced a tree, cooled his hot cheek on the bark, and the night winds eagerly absorbed the breath which restlessly pressed forward from his pure breast. He felt for the scarf that he had had from her and taken away with him, it had been forgotten, it was in the clothing he had had on earlier. His lips were parched, his limbs trembled with desire.

The music stopped, and he felt as if he had fallen out of the element in which his feelings had been carried hitherto. His disquiet increased, since his emotions were no longer being nurtured and softened by the gentle tones. He sat down on the doorstep, and already felt more composed. He kissed the brass ring with which one knocked at her door, he kissed the threshold over which her feet went in and out, and warmed it with the fire of his breast. Then he sat still for a while longer and thought of her as being behind her curtains in the white nightdress with the red ribbon round her head in sweet repose, and thought of himself as being so close to her that it seemed to him that she would now have to dream of him. His thoughts were affectionate, like the spirits of twilight; quiet and disquiet alternated within him; with shuddering hand love coursed thousandfold over all the strings of his soul; it was as if the music of the spheres was pausing above him in order to listen to the quiet melodies of his heart.

If he had had the front-door key with him, which at other times opened Mariane's door to him, he would not have restrained himself, he would have penetrated into the sanctuary of love. But he went away slowly, making his way unsteadily and half in a dream among the trees; he wanted to go home, and yet again and again felt that he was being turned back; finally, when he could bring himself to it, and when he went and looked back at the corner once more, it seemed to him as if Mariane's door were being opened and a dark figure were coming out. He was too far off to see clearly, and before he could pull himself together and look up properly, the manifestation was already lost again in the night; only in the far distance did he believe he could see it again, slipping past a white house. He stood and blinked, and before he could pull himself together and give chase, the phantom had disappeared. Where should he follow it to? What street had absorbed the man, if that was what it was?

Just as someone for whom a flash of lightning has lit up the area in one corner looks in vain with dazzled eyes immediately afterwards for earlier shapes and the relationship of the paths, so it was before Wilhelm's eyes and in his heart. And just as a midnight ghost which causes enormous fears is considered in the following moments of self-control to be a child of terror and the dreadful apparition leaves doubts without end in the mind, so Wilhelm also was in the greatest agitation when, leaning on a corner-stone, he paid no attention to the brightness of the morning and the crowing of the cocks until early working activities started to come to life and drove him home.

When he was back, he had almost banished the unexpected delusive occurrence from his mind by means of the most telling arguments; yet the happy night mood, which he now thought back to also only as if it were something imaginary, had gone too. In order to assuage his heart and to put a seal upon his returning faith, he took the scarf out of the pocket of the clothes he had been wearing previously. The sound of a note falling out caused him to remove the scarf from his lips; he lifted it up and read:

'Oh, how I love you, you little fool! What was up with you yesterday? I am coming to you tonight. I can quite believe that you will be sorry to go away from here; but be patient; I shall come after you to the fair. Listen, don't put on the black, green and brown coat for me, it makes you look like the witch of Endor. Have I not sent you the white négligé because I want to hold a little white lamb in my arms? Send me your notes as usual via old Sibyl; the devil himself has chosen the role of Iris for her.'

BOOK TWO

Chapter One

Anyone who makes energetic efforts before our eyes with a view to attaining a goal, can be assured of our sympathy, whether we approve or disapprove of his aim; but as soon as the matter has been decided, we at once turn our glance away from him; what has been finished and laid aside can in no wise attract our attention, especially if already at an early stage we have prophesied a bad outcome for the undertaking.

For this reason our readers are not to be provided in detail with an account of the misery and distress which befell our unfortunate friend, when he saw his hopes and wishes destroyed in so unexpected a manner. On the contrary we shall pass over a few years and not seek him out again until we can hope to find him involved in a kind of activity and enjoyment, after we have given just a brief account of as much as is necessary to ensure the coherence of the story.

The plague or a malignant fever rage more quickly and more violently in a healthy and fully sound body which they attack, and so poor Wilhelm was unexpectedly overcome by an unhappy fate, so that in *one* moment his whole being was disturbed. As when by chance a firework catches fire among the prepared equipment and the shells which have been artfully bored and filled and which, after being ordered and let off according to a certain plan, should sketch a magnificent sequence of fire-pictures in the air, now hiss and rush untidily and dangerously in confusion, so now happiness and hope, pleasure and joy, reality and dream were all at once thrown pell-mell together, foundering in his heart. In such desolate moments the friend who rushes |up to be of help feels benumbed, and for the one who is affected it is a kindness that his senses leave him.

Days of vocal, eternally recurrent and intentionally renewed grief followed; but these are also to be considered as a favour of nature. In such hours Wilhelm had not yet quite lost his beloved; his sufferings were tirelessly renewed attempts to hold fast still to the happiness that had disappeared from his soul, to seize once more the possibility of this happiness, and to procure a short after-life for his joys that had departed for ever. Just as a body cannot be called wholly dead as long as putrefaction continues, and as long as the forces which endeavour in vain to function according to their old purposes toil away at the destruction of the parts to which they formerly brought life; so only when everything has been worn down and we see the whole reduced to indifferent dust, does the pitiful, empty feeling of death arise in us, to be revived only by the breath of Him who lives eternally.

In such a fresh, untrammelled, likeable temperament there was much that could be lacerated, destroyed and smothered, and the quickly healing strength of youth gave new sustenance and intensity to the violence of the grief. The blow had struck his whole being at the roots. Werner, of necessity his confidant, zealously took up fire and sword in order to penetrate into the innermost life of the monster, a hated passion. The opportunity was so favourable, the proof so close to hand, and there were so many stories and tales that he could use. He did this step by step with such intensity and ferocity, did not leave his friend the comfort of the slightest momentary deception, and barred him the way to any hiding-place where he might have been able to save himself from despair, that nature, unwilling for her darling to perish, beset him with sickness, so that there could be release for him from the other side.

A high fever with its after-effects, medicines, excessive tension and exhaustion, then the efforts of the family and the love of his contemporaries which makes itself especially felt in deprivation and need, were so many distractions to a changed mental state and were scanty entertainment. It was not until he was becoming better again, that is, when his strength was exhausted, that Wilhelm looked down in terror at the painful abyss of desolate wretchedness, like someone peering down into the burnt-out, hollow crater of a volcano.

Then he reproached himself most bitterly that after such a great loss he could experience any further painless, quiet and indifferent moments. He despised his own heart and yearned for the consolation of wretchedness and tears.

In order to re-awaken his tears, he recalled to his mind all the scenes of past happiness. With the utmost vividness he imagined them and endeavoured to recapture them, and when he had worked his way upwards as far as possible and when the sunshine of earlier days seemed to be animating his limbs and lifting his heart, he looked back to the terrible abyss, took comfort for his eyes from the destructive depths, hurled himself down and wrested from nature the bitterest sufferings. He lacerated himself with cruelty repeated in this way; for youth, so rich in hidden strength, does not realize what it is squandering when it adds on to the grief caused by a loss still further forced sufferings, as if it were only by this means that what was lost would acquire real value. Furthermore, he was so convinced that this loss was the only one, the first and the last, that he could experience in his life that he abhorred any consolation which undertook to present these sufferings to him as finite.

Chapter Two

Accustomed to tormenting himself in this way, he now also attacked the remaining element, which had given him the greatest joys and hopes after and with love, his gift as poet and actor, with spiteful criticism and from all angles. In his writings he saw nothing but a mindless imitation of a few traditional forms, without inner value; he was only willing to recognize them as stiff school exercises that were lacking any spark of naturalness, truth and enthusiasm. All he could find in his poems was a monotonous metrical form in which quite commonplace thoughts and emotions dragged themselves along, held together by wretched rhyming; and in this way he also deprived himself in that field of any prospect and pleasure that could possibly have restored him again.

His acting talent did not fare better. He chided himself for not having discovered earlier the vanity which, he thought, alone lay at the basis of this presumption. His figure, his walk, his movements and declamation had to pay for this; he denied decisively to himself every kind of preference and any service that might have raised him up above the commonplace, and by this he increased his mute despair to the highest degree. For if it is hard to renounce a woman's love, it does not feel any the less painful to wrench oneself away from the company of the Muses, to declare oneself to be eternally unworthy of their companionship and to dispense with the finest and closest applause which is given to our person, our behaviour and our voice in public.

In this way our friend had become fully resigned and had at the same time been devoting himself with great zeal to business affairs. To the surprise of his friend and to the greatest satisfaction of his father, no one was more active than he in the counting-house and stock exchange, in shop and cellar; he dealt with and disposed of correspondence and accounts, and whatever he was asked to do, with the greatest industry and keenness. Admittedly, not with the cheerful industry, which is at the same time reward in itself for the busy person, when we accomplish that which we were born for with orderliness and consequentiality, but with the quiet conscientiousness of duty which is motivated by the best intentions and is nurtured by conviction and rewarded by inner self-esteem; but which none the less can often scarcely stifle an importunate sigh, even when it is being crowned by the finest state of awareness.

Wilhelm had gone on living in this way very busily for a time and had convinced himself that that hard testing by fate had been arranged for his own good. He was glad to see himself warned in good time, albeit in an unfriendly enough way, on the way of life, whereas others make amends later and under greater stress for the blunders to which a youthful presumption has misled them. For usually man fights as long as he can against sending the fool packing whom he cherishes in his heart, against admitting a major error and confessing a truth that drives him to despair.

Decided as he was to renounce his fondest imaginings, some time was none the less necessary in order to convince him completely about his misfortune. At last, however, he had so fully destroyed within himself all hope of love, of poetic creation and of personal performance by means of telling arguments that he plucked up the courage to extinguish completely all traces of his folly and everything that could still remind him of it. He had therefore lit a fire in a grate one cool evening and fetched out a reliquary containing all kinds of bagatelles which he had received or stolen from Mariane at significant moments. Each dried flower reminded him of the time when it was still freshly blooming in her hair, each note reminded him of the happy hour to which she was thereby inviting him, each bow recalled that fond resting-place of his head, her beautiful bosom. Was not each motion, which for a long time now he had believed dead, in this way compelled to begin to come to life again? Was not the passion which he had mastered when separated from his beloved compelled to grow strong again in the presence of these mementoes? For we do not notice how sad and unpleasant a dull day is until a single, penetrating ray of sunshine portrays for us the cheering brightness of a clear afternoon.

He was, therefore, not unmoved to see these relics which had been kept for so long go up one after the other in smoke and flames. Several times he paused hesitatingly and he still had a string of pearls and a floral scarf left over when he decided to liven up the dying fire with the poetic attempts of his youth.

Up to now he had carefully preserved everything that he had written, from the earliest period of his mind's development onward. His writings still lay in bundles at the bottom of the trunk where he had packed them at the time when he was hoping to take them with him on his flight. In how different a mood did he open them now from the time when he had tied them together!

If we open at some time later a letter, which we wrote and sealed up in particular circumstances, but which does not reach the friend to whom it was directed and is returned to us, a strange emotion overcomes us when we break open our own seal and converse with our changed self as with a third person. A similar feeling seized hold of our friend with intensity when he opened the first package and threw on to the fire the copy-books after they had been split up; they were just flaring up violently when Werner entered and, surprised at the lively flames, asked what was going on.

'I am providing a proof,' said Wilhelm, 'that I am serious about giving up a craft for which I was not born'; and with these words he threw the second package into the fire. Werner tried to stop him, but it was too late.

'I don't see why you need take this extreme step,' the latter said. 'Why ever now should these pieces of work be destroyed, even if they are not outstanding?'

'Because a poem ought either to be first-rate or not to exist at all; because everybody who does not have the gift of producing the best should refrain from creative art and be seriously wary of any temptation towards it. For admittedly there stirs in every human being a certain undefined desire to imitate what he sees; but this desire by no means proves that there also dwells in us the strength to do justice to what we undertake. Just look at the way boys walk to and fro and do balancing acts on every plank and beam whenever the tightrope-walkers are in the town, until some other stimulus leads them away to some comparable form of play again. Haven't you noticed it in the circle of your friends? Whenever a musical virtuoso is to be heard, there are always people who at once start to learn the same instrument. How many go astray on this path! Happy is the man who is quick to become aware of the false conclusion from his wishes to his ability!'

Werner contradicted; the conversation became lively, and Wilhelm could not repeat to his friend without emotion the arguments with which he had tormented himself so often. Werner maintained that it was not sensible to give up completely a talent for which one only had moderate inclination and ability because one would never put it into practice to the fullest perfection. After all there was so much spare time that could be filled by such a talent, and gradually there would come the possibility of producing something by means of which we could bring pleasure to ourselves and to others.

Our friend, who held a quite contrary opinion about this, at once interrupted him, and said with great vivacity:

'How wrong you are, dear friend, if you believe that a piece of work whose first conception must fill the whole soul, can be produced in interrupted hours and in units of time that have been stingily scraped together. No, the poet must live completely for *himself,* wholly in his beloved themes. He who is inwardly endowed by heaven in the rarest manner, and who preserves in his bosom a treasure which continually increases, must live also outwardly undisturbed with his treasures in a quiet bliss which a rich man vainly tries to induce around himself by means of piled-up material goods. Look how people chase after happiness and pleasure! Their wishes, their efforts and their money hunt restlessly—for what? For what the poet has received from nature, for the enjoyment of the world, for sympathetic identification of himself in others, for harmonious unity with many things that are often irreconcilable.

'What disturbs people, is not that they cannot connect their ideas with things, that pleasure eludes their grasp, that what is yearned for comes too late and that everything acquired and attained fails to have the effect on their heart which desire from a distance causes us to anticipate. Fate has set the poet up above all this as if he were a god. He can see the vain turmoil of the confusion of passions, families and kingdoms, he can see how insoluble enigmas of misunderstanding, which often only need a monosyllabic word for their unravelling, are the cause of ineffably harmful confusions. He can have sympathy with the sadness and the joy of every human fate. While the man of the world drags out his days in a consuming melancholy because of a great loss or else moves towards his destiny in wild gaiety, the receptive and sensitive soul of the poet steps onward like the sun in its progress from night to day, and his harp makes gentle modulations to be in tune with happiness and suffering. Native to his heart's ground, the beautiful flower of wisdom grows forth, and if others live in a waking dream and are terrified out of their senses by monstrous imaginings, he lives the dream of life as one who is awake, and the strangest thing that happens is for him at once past and future. And thus the poet is at one and the same time teacher, soothsayer, and friend of gods and men. What! Do you want him to descend to some wretched trade? He who is built like a bird to hover over the world, to make his home on high peaks and to take his food from buds and fruit, easily confusing one branch with another—should he at the same time pull at the plough like the ox, get used to a trail like a dog, or perhaps even be tied to a chain and protect a farm with his barking?'

Werner had listened with astonishment, as can be imagined. 'If only human beings were made like birds,' he interposed, 'and could pass gracious days in constant pleasure, without spinning and weaving! If only they too could go as easily into distant regions at the coming of winter, to avoid want and to safeguard themselves against frost!'

'That is the way poets lived in times when what was admirable was more easily recognized,' Wilhelm cried out, 'and that is how they always ought to live. Sufficiently provided for in their inner selves, they needed little from outside; from time immemorial the gift of presenting beautiful emotions and magnificent images to people in sweet words and melodies which cover all subjects has entranced the world and has been a plenteous hereditary portion for the gifted person. At the courts of kings, at the tables of the rich, outside the doors of those in love people listened to them, with their ears and mind closed to all else, just as we count ourselves fortunate and stand still with delight when the voice of the nightingale with its stupendous emotional force comes forth from the bushes through which we are walking! They found a hospitable world, and their lowly seeming status only raised them the more. The hero listened to their songs, and the world conqueror paid tribute to the poet because he felt that without him his mighty existence would only pass by like the wind of a storm; the lover wished to feel his desire and his pleasure so many times and in so harmonious a manner as the inspired poetic lips could describe them; and even the rich man could not see his own possessions and idols with his own eyes as so precious as they appeared to him after they had been illuminated by the brilliance of a mind that could appreciate and intensify all value. Yes, if you like, who apart from the poet has formed gods, has elevated us to them, and brought them down to us?'

'My friend,' Werner replied after some thought, 'I have already often regretted that you strive to banish forcibly from your soul what you feel so keenly. I should be making a great mistake, if it were not better for you to give way to yourself to some extent rather than to worry yourself to death through the conflicts of such a harsh abjuration and, by depriving yourself of *one* innocent joy, take away from yourself the pleasure of all the rest.'

'Dare I confess to you, my friend,' the other said, 'and I hope you won't find me ridiculous, when I admit to you that those images still pursue me, however much I flee from them, and that when I look into my heart all early wishes are lodged there firmly, even more firmly than usual? But in my wretchedness what else can I do at present? Ah, if anyone had predicted to me that the arms of my spirit, with which I stretched into infinity and with which I certainly hoped to grasp something great, would be shattered so soon, he would have driven me to despair. And even now when judgment has been passed on me, when I have lost *her* who, instead of a deity, was to have led me to the fulfilment of my wishes, what else remains for me to do except to yield to the bitterest griefs? Oh, my brother,' he continued, 'I do not deny that in my secret calculations she was the block to which a rope-ladder is affixed; the adventurer sways in the air, hoping in the midst of danger, the iron breaks, and he lies shattered at the foot of his aspirations. There is no longer any consolation or hope for me either! I shan't let a single one of these unfortunate papers remain,' he exclaimed, leaping to his feet. Once more he seized a few copybooks, tore them apart and threw them on to the fire. Werner tried to stop him, but in vain. 'Leave me!' Wilhelm cried, 'what use are these miserable pages? For me they are no longer a step forward nor an encouragement. Are they to remain extant in order to torment me until the end of my life? Are they perhaps one day to be a mockery to the world, instead of arousing pity and terror? How wretched I am and how wretched is my fate! Now for the first time I understand the laments of the poets, those sad people who have become wise out of necessity. How long did I consider myself indestructible and invulnerable, and, alas, I now see that a deep injury inflicted at an early stage cannot grow out again and restore itself; I feel that I must take it with me into the grave. No! For no day of my life is the grief, which will finally kill me, to leave my side, and the thought of *her* is to stay with me, to live and to die with me, the thought of someone who is unworthy—ah, my friend! If I am to speak from the heart—of someone who is certainly not wholly unworthy! Her profession and what has happened to her have excused her a thousand times over, in my estimation. I was too cruel, you were merciless in initiating me into your own coldness and hardness, you took my unnerved senses prisoner and stopped me from doing for her and for myself what I owed to both of us. Who knows what a state I may have put her in, and it is only gradually that the despair and helplessness I have left her in weighs upon my conscience! Wasn't it possible that she had a good excuse? Wasn't it possible? How many misunderstandings can confuse the world, how many circumstances can implore forgiveness for the greatest fault!—How often I picture her to myself, sitting quietly on her own, leaning on her elbows! "That is the fidelity and love which he swore to me!" she is saying. "To end the sweet life that bound us together with this harsh blow!" '—He burst into a flood of tears, throwing his face forward on to the table and moistening the remaining papers.

Werner stood by in the greatest embarrassment. He had not suspected this rapid flare-up of passion. At times he tried to interrupt his friend's speech, at times to deflect the conversation to another subject, but in vain, he could not withstand the flow. Here also the lasting friendship again assumed responsibility. He let the stormiest attack of grief take its course while through his quiet presence he best made visible his honest, unalloyed sympathy, and so they remained on that evening: Wilhelm plunged into the quiet aftermath of grief, and his friend terrified at the fresh outburst of a passion which he believed had been conquered a long time ago and which he had overwhelmed with good advice and zealous entreaties.

Chapter Three

After such relapses Wilhelm was mostly accustomed to devoting himself all the more keenly to business affairs and activity, and it was the best way of escaping from the labyrinth that was trying to allure him once more. His good way of behaving with strangers and the facility with which he could correspond in almost all living languages gave his father and the latter's business partner ever more hope and consoled them with regard to the illness whose cause they did not know and with regard to the interval of time which had interrupted their plan. Wilhelm's departure was decided upon a second time, and we find him on his horse, his valise behind him, cheered by fresh air and movement as he approaches the mountainous region where he should be carrying out some commissions.

He roamed slowly through valleys and mountains with the sensation of the greatest pleasure. Here for the first time he saw overhanging rocks, rushing streams, overgrown cliff-faces and deep valleys, and yet his earliest youthful dreams had already haunted such areas. He felt rejuvenated at the sight of these things, all the troubles that he had suffered had been washed away from his soul, and in complete cheerfulness he recited to himself passages from various poems, in particular from the *Pastor fido*[1], and these passages swam in shoals into his memory, especially when he was at these lonely spots. He also remembered many passages from songs of his own which he recited with particular contentment. He populated the world which lay before him with all sorts of figures from the past, and every step that he took into the future was for him full of the presentiment of important actions and strange occurrences.

Several people, who came up behind him one after the other, passed him with a greeting and hurriedly continued their way into the mountains on steep footpaths, interrupted his quiet communing a number of times, though without his having paid attention to them. Finally a conversational traveller attached himself to him and narrated the reason for the numerous pilgrims.

'At Hochdorf this evening there's going to be a play,' he said, 'and the whole neighbourhood has been assembling for it.'

'What!' cried Wilhelm. 'has the art of drama found a way and built itself a temple in these lonely mountains, between these impenetrable forests? And I must make my pilgrimage to its festival?'

'You'll be even more surprised,' the other man said, 'when you hear who is putting on the play. There's a big factory in the place which feeds a lot of people. The entrepreneur who so to speak lives remote from all human society knows of no better way to occupy his workers in the winter than to get them to act plays. He won't tolerate any card-playing amongst them and in general wishes to restrain them from coarse manners. This is the way they spend the long evenings, and as it's the old man's birthday today, they are presenting a particular festivity in his honour.'

Wilhelm arrived in Hochdorf, where he was supposed to be spending the night, and dismounted by the factory whose owner was also on his list of debtors.

When he heard his name, the old man exclaimed in astonishment: 'Well, sir, are you the son of the good man to whom I owe so much gratitude and up to the present money as well? Your father has had so much patience with me that I would have to be

1. *Pastor fido,* pastoral drama by Giovanni Battista Guarini, first published 1590. (Tr.)

a villain if I did not pay promptly and cheerfully. You've come just at the right time to see that I'm in earnest about it.'

He summoned his wife, who was equally pleased to see the young man; she gave the assurance that he was like his father, and regretted that she could not give him hospitality for the night because of the many visitors.

The business matter was straightforward and was soon settled; Wilhelm put a rouleau of gold into his pocket and hoped that the rest of his business affairs would go as smoothly.

The hour for the play was drawing near; they were only waiting now for the chief forester, who at last also arrived with some huntsmen and was received with the greatest respect.

The company was now ushered into the playhouse, for which purpose a barn lying close to the garden had been adapted. Without particular taste the building and the theatre had been prepared brightly and pleasantly enough. One of the painters who worked at the factory had worked as a handyman at the court-theatre and had now put up forest, street and indoor sets, admittedly in rather rough fashion. They had borrowed the play from an itinerant troupe and had re-arranged it to suit themselves. The way it was, was entertaining. The plot, in which two lovers attempted to wrest a girl from her guardian and alternatively from each other, gave rise to all sorts of interesting situations. It was the first play that our friend had seen again after such a long period; he made a number of observations. It was full of action, but without portrayal of real characters. It gave pleasure and amusement. The beginnings of all theatrical art are like this. A rough fellow is content so long as he can see something happening; an educated person wishes to be moved in his feelings, and only the fully cultivated man finds reflective thought pleasant.

He would have liked to have given some help to the actors here and there; for it only wanted a little for them to have been quite a lot better.

The smell of tobacco, becoming even stronger, disturbed him in his quiet considerations. Soon after the beginning of the play the chief forester had lit his pipe, and gradually several people took this liberty. What is more, this gentleman's large dogs caused disagreeable scenes. They had been locked out; but they soon found the way in by the rear door, mounted the stage, ran up against the actors and finally took a leap across the orchestra to join their master who had taken the front seat in the auditorium.

As epilogue a tribute was presented. A portrait depicting the old man dressed in his bridegroom's attire stood on an altar, hung with wreaths. All the actors paid homage to it in humble postures.

The youngest child, dressed in white, stepped forward and made a speech in verse which moved the whole family to tears and indeed also the chief forester who was reminded of his own children. Thus the play ended, and Wilhelm could not restrain himself from going behind the scenes, seeing the actresses close to, complimenting them on their performance and giving them some advice for the future.

Our friend's other business calls which he gradually dealt with in fairly large and fairly small mountain localities did not all take their course so happily or so pleasurably. Many debtors asked for a postponement, many were impolite, many made denials. Following the instructions given to him, he was to sue some of them; he had to visit and instruct a solicitor, appear before the court of justice, and undertake whatever other tiresome duties might be required.

Things went just as badly for him when people wanted to do him an honour. He only found a few people who could give him some sort of useful instruction; there were only few with whom he could hope to take up a profitable business relationship. As now also, unfortunately, rainy weather set in and as a journey by horse was linked with unbearable difficulties in these regions, he thanked heaven when he approached level ground again, and saw at the foot of the mountain in a beautiful and fertile plain by the gentle river in the sunlight a cheerful little country town in which, it was true, he had no business dealings, but for that very reason he decided to spend a few days there, in order to provide some respite for himself and his horse, which had suffered considerably from the bad roads.

Chapter Four

When he entered an inn by the market, things were going very merrily there, or at least in a very lively manner. A large company of tightrope-walkers, jumpers and jugglers, who had a strong man with them, had come in, accompanied by wives and children, and while preparing for a public appearance were causing one piece of nonsense after another. Now they argued with the innkeeper, now among themselves; and if their quarrelling was unbearable, their expressions of pleasure were completely intolerable. Undecided whether to go or stay, he paused at the door and looked at the workmen who were beginning to put up a scaffolding on the market-place.

A girl with roses and other flowers offered him her basket, and he bought a pretty bunch which he rearranged differently according to his fancy and then looked at with satisfaction, when the window of another inn which stood at the side of the square opened, and a well-appointed lady showed herself at this window. In spite of the distance he could note that a pleasant cheerfulness animated her face. Her blonde hair fell negligently about her neck; she seemed to be looking round for the stranger. A little later a boy with a hairdresser's apron and a little white jacket stepped out of the door of that building, approached Wilhelm, greeted him and said: 'The lady at the window would like to ask whether you would be willing to forego to her some of the lovely flowers.'—'They are all at her service', Wilhelm replied, handing the small messenger the bouquet and at the same time bowing to the beautiful woman; she replied to the gesture with a friendly greeting in return and withdrew from the window.

Reflecting on this pleasant adventure, he was going up the stairs to his room when a young creature who drew his attention to her leapt towards him. A little short silk waistcoat with slit Spanish-style sleeves and long close-fitting trousers with puffs looked very well on the child. Long black hair had been set in curls and plaits and wound round her hair. He looked at the figure in astonishment and could not make up his mind whether he should declare it to be a boy or a girl. However, he soon decided on the latter, and stopped her as she was passing him, said 'good day' to her and asked her to whom she belonged, although he could easily see that she must be a member of the troupe of acrobats and dancers. She looked at him with a sharp, black-eyed side-glance, and at the same time disengaged herself from him and ran into the kitchen without replying.

When he came up the stairs he found two men in the extensive ante-room who were performing fencing exercises or rather seemed to be vying with each other in skills. The one evidently belonged to the troupe which was in the house, whereas the other had a less wild appearance. Wilhelm looked at them and had reason to admire both; and when the black-bearded, sinewy fighter not long after left the scene of action, the other man offered the rapier to Wilhelm with much civility.

'If you are willing to put a pupil through his paces,' the latter replied, 'I am indeed happy to venture a few passes with you.' They fenced together, and although the stranger was far superior to the one who had just arrived, he was none the less polite enough to assure him that it was all a matter of practice; and indeed Wilhelm had also shown that he had earlier been trained by a good, thorough German fencing-master.

Their occupation was interrupted by the noise with which the motley company set out from the inn in order to inform the town about their show and to make people eager to see their arts. A drummer was followed by the entrepreneur on horseback, behind him came a woman-dancer on a similar nag holding a child who was brightly decked out with ribbons and tinsel. After that came the rest of the troupe on foot, some of whom were carrying children on their shoulders easily and comfortably in unusual positions, and among them the young, black-haired, sombre figure again caught Wilhelm's attention.

The clown ran amusingly this way and that among the thronging crowd and distributed his leaflets together with very intelligible jokes, as now he kissed a girl and now he hit a boy with his slapstick, awakening in the people an irresistible impulse to get to know him better.

In the printed notices the varied arts of the company, in particular of a Monsieur Narcissus and a Demoiselle Landrinette, had been extolled; these two, as principal characters, had had the shrewdness not to take part in the procession, and thereby to give themselves a greater appearance of distinction and to arouse more curiosity.

During the procession the lovely neighbour had also shown herself at the window again, and Wilhelm had not failed to inquire about her from his companion. The latter, whom for the time being we will call Laertes, offered to escort Wilhelm over to her. 'The lady and myself', he said with a smile, 'are two remnants of a company of actors that disbanded here a short time ago. The pleasantness of the place has persuaded us to stay here a while and to consume in peace our little remaining cash that was collected, while a friend has set off in search of employment for himself and for us.'

Laertes at once accompanied his new acquaintance to Philine's door, where he left him waiting a moment, so that he could get some sweets in a nearby shop. 'I'm sure you will be grateful to me for procuring you this agreeable connection', he said when he came back.

The lady stepped towards them out of the room on a pair of light slippers with high heels. She had thrown a black mantilla over a white négligé which, because it was not completely clean, gave her a domesticated and comfortable appearance; her short skirt allowed the prettiest feet in the world to be seen.

'Pleased to meet you,' she called to Wilhelm, 'and let me thank you for the beautiful flowers.' She led him into the room with one hand, while she pressed the bunch of flowers to her breast with the other. When they had sat down and had become engaged in trivial conversation, to which she was able to give a charming turn, Laertes poured out roasted almonds into her lap, and at once she started eating them. 'See what a child this young person is', she exclaimed: 'he will try to persuade you that I am a great friend of such dainties, whereas it is *he* who can't live without enjoying something tasty.'

'Just let us confess,' rejoined Laertes, 'that we like to keep each other company in this, as in various other things. For instance,' he said, 'it is a very pleasant day today; I think we might go for a drive and take lunch at the Mill.'—'Gladly,' said Philine, 'we must provide our new friend with a little variety.' Laertes rushed away, for he never simply went, and Wilhelm wanted to go for a moment to his own quarters, in order to have his hair tidied up, for it still looked dishevelled from the journey. 'You can do that here,' she said, called her little servant and pressed Wilhelm in the most charming manner to take off his coat, to put on her peignoir and to have his hair dressed in her presence. 'You must never lose time,' she said; 'you never know how long we shall be together.'

The boy, sulky and resentful rather than clumsy, was not on his best behaviour; he pulled at Wilhelm's hair and seemed to be unwilling to finish as quickly as all that. Philine reproved him several times for his rudeness, finally pushing him impatiently away and chasing him out of the room. She now undertook the work herself and curled our friend's hair with great facility and delicacy, although she too did not seem to be in a hurry and found fault with her own handiwork, now for this reason, now for that, and at the same time she could not avoid touching his knees with hers and bringing flowers and bosom so near to his lips that he was tempted more than once to implant a kiss there.

When Wilhelm had cleaned his brow with a little powder-knife, she said to him: 'Take it and remember me in doing so.' It was a good knife; the hilt of inlaid steel displayed the friendly words: 'Remember me'. Wilhelm put it away, thanked her and asked permission to be allowed to give her a little present in return.

Now they were ready. Laertes had brought the coach, and now a very merry journey began. Philine threw something from the carriage-door to every poor person who begged of them, at the same time calling to the beggar a cheerful and friendly remark.

They had scarcely reached the Mill and ordered a meal when

music was to be heard outside the building. There were miners who recited various agreeable songs with lively, strident voices to the accompaniment of zither and triangle. It was not long before a crowd came up and formed a circle round them, and the company at the inn nodded approvingly to them from the windows. Having seen this attention to them they extended their circle and seemed to be preparing for their most important item. After a pause a miner stepped forward with a pick and, while the others were playing a serious melody, he mimed the action of digging.

It was not long before a farmer stepped forward from the crowd and indicated to the miner with pantomimic threats that he should move away from here. The onlookers were surprised at this and did not recognize the miner who was disguised as a farmer until he opened his mouth and in a kind of recitative scolded the other man for daring to busy himself on his ground. The former did not lose his composure, but began to teach the countryman that he was right to strike into the earth here, and in so doing gave him the first principle of mining work. The farmer, who did not understand the strange terminology, put all kinds of silly questions at which the audience, thinking itself cleverer, burst into hearty laughter. The miner tried to instruct him and demonstrated to him the advantages that would in the end also reach him, if the subterranean treasures of the land were burrowed out. The farmer, who at first had threatened the other man with blows, let himself gradually be calmed down, and they separated as good friends; the miner in particular came out of this altercation most creditably.

'From this little dialogue,' said Wilhelm at table, 'we have the most striking example of how useful the theatre could be to all walks of life, of how much advantage the state would derive from it, if the actions, professions and ventures of people were brought on to the stage from their good, praiseworthy side and bearing in mind the point of view from which the state itself must honour and protect them. At the moment we only depict the ridiculous side of people; the writer of comedy is as it were only a malicious inspector who everywhere has a watchful eye for the failings of his fellow-citizens and seems to be pleased when he can make something stick on them. Would it not be a pleasant and worthwhile undertaking for a statesman to survey the natural, mutual influence of all classes and to direct a poet, who had sufficient ability, at his work? I am convinced that in this way many very absorbing and at the same time useful and amusing plays could be created.'

'As far as I have been able to see,' said Laertes, 'wherever I have been on my wanderings, people can only prohibit, hinder and reject; but only rarely can they command, encourage and reward. Everything is acceptable until it becomes harmful; then people get angry and hit out.'

'Let's forget the state and the statesmen,' said Philine, 'I can't imagine them except in wigs, and a wig, no matter who is wearing it, arouses a frantic movement of my fingers; I should like to pull it off the venerable gentleman, leap around the room and laugh at the bald head.'

Philine broke off the conversation by singing some lively songs, which she did very pleasantly, and she urged them to a quick return so that they would not miss seeing the arts of the acrobats in the evening. Droll to the point of boisterousness, she continued her generosity to the poor on the homeward journey until, since she and her travelling companions had run out of money, she threw out her straw hat to a girl and her neckerchief to an old woman.

Philine invited both her companions into her apartment because, as she said, the public performance could be seen better from her windows than from the other inn.

When they arrived, they found the scaffolding in place and the background decorated with hanging tapestries. The spring-boards had already been put in place, the slack rope fastened to the posts and the tight rope drawn over the trestles. The square was fairly full of people and the windows were occupied by spectators of some quality.

The clown first of all prepared the gathering to attentiveness and good humour with some silly tricks which always make the audience laugh. Some children, whose bodies portrayed the strangest dislocations, aroused now astonishment and now horror, and Wilhelm could not refrain from feeling intense pity when he saw the child, for whom he had felt sympathy at first sight, performing the strange postures with some effort. But soon the amusing acrobats aroused lively pleasure as they turned somersaults first individually, then one behind the other and finally all together, forwards and backwards. Loud clapping and cheering resounded from the whole gathering.

But now attention was directed to a completely different subject. One after another the children had to step on to the rope, the novices first, so that they could lengthen the performance by their exercises and highlight the difficulties of the art. Some men and adult females performed with some skill; but they were not yet Monsieur Narcissus nor Demoiselle Landrinette.

At last the latter also stepped forward from a kind of tent behind outstretched red curtains, and with their pleasant figures and smart finery fulfilled the hitherto happily nurtured hopes of the audience: he, a cheery little fellow of moderate size, with black eyes and a strong pigtail; she, no less well developed and strong; both displayed themselves in turn on the tight-rope with light movements, leaps and strange postures. Her daintiness and his boldness, and the precision with which both executed their clever tricks, heightened the general pleasure at each step and leap they took. The dignity of their behaviour, the apparent efforts of the others around them gave them the appearance of being lord and master of the whole troupe, and everyone thought them worthy of this rank.

The enthusiasm of the crowd spread to the onlookers at the windows, the ladies looked constantly at Narcissus, the gentlemen at Landrinette. The crowd shouted with joy, and the more elegant public did not refrain from clapping; they scarcely laughed at the clown any longer. Only a few crept away when some members of the troupe pressed through the crowd with tin plates in order to collect money.

'They've done their job well, it seems to me,' Wilhelm said to Philine who was with him at the window; 'I admire the intelligence with which they could give meaning even to little turns, brought forward gradually and at the right time, and the way they fused together from the clumsiness of their children and the virtuosity of their best people a totality which in the first place attracted our attention and then entertained us most agreeably.'

Gradually the crowd had dispersed and the square had become empty, while Philine and Laertes disputed about the skills of Narcissus and Landrinette and teased each other. Wilhelm saw the strange child standing in the street by other children who were playing, and pointed her out to Philine who at once, in her lively manner, called to the child and beckoned, and since she did not want to come, clattered down the stairs singing and led her up.

'Here's the little enigma,' she cried as she brought the child to the door. The latter stood by the entrance, just as if she would like to slip out again straightaway, placed her right hand on her breast, her left hand before her brow and bowed deeply. 'Don't be afraid, little one,' Wilhelm said, moving towards her. She looked at him with an uncertain glance and stepped a few paces nearer.

'What's your name?' he asked.—'They call me Mignon.'—'How old are you?'—'Nobody has counted the years.'—'Who was your father?'—'The big devil's dead.'

'Well, that's strange enough!' exclaimed Philine. They asked her a few more questions; she articulated her replies in broken German and in a particularly solemn manner; in so doing, she each time placed her hands on her breast and head and bowed deeply.

Wilhelm could not look at her enough. His eyes and his heart were irresistibly fascinated by the mysterious condition of this being. He estimated her as being twelve or thirteen years old; she had a good physique, except that her limbs promised stronger growth or else announced a development that was retarded. Her features were not regular, but striking; her brow mysterious, her nose extraordinary beautiful, and her mouth, although it seemed too firmly closed for her age and at times she twitched her lips to one side, still candid and attractive enough. Her brownish complexion could scarcely be recognized through the make-up. This figure made a deep impression on Wilhelm; he kept on looking at her, fell silent and forgot her presence because of his reflections. Philine aroused him from his half-dream when she gave the child some of the sweets that were left over and signalled to her to withdraw. She made her bow, as earlier on, and rushed quick as lightning out of the door.

When the time now approached for our new acquaintances to separate for that evening, they arranged first to go for a drive together on the next day. They once more wanted to take lunch at another place, at a nearby hunting-lodge. Wilhelm had quite a lot more to say in praise of Philine that evening, but Laertes' replies were only brief and flippant.

The next morning, when they had again had an hour's fencing practice, they went to Philine's inn; they had already seen the hired carriage drawn up outside. But how surprised Wilhelm was to find that the carriage had disappeared, and how much more so when he found that Philine was not present. She had sat down in the coach with some strangers who had arrived that morning, it was reported, and had driven off with them. Our friend, who had promised himself pleasant entertainment in her company, could not conceal his annoyance. Laertes, on the other hand, laughed out loud and cried: 'That's how I like her! It's just like her! Let us simply go straight to the hunting-lodge; let her be wherever she likes, we don't want to miss our outing on her account.'

While they were on their way, Wilhelm continued to censure this inconsistency of behaviour, and Laertes said: 'I can't find it inconsistent when somebody remains true to his character. When she undertakes something or promises something to somebody, it is only on the tacit understanding that it will also be convenient for her to carry out the intention or to keep her promise. She likes to give presents, but you always have to be ready to give her the present back.'

'She's a strange character,' interposed Wilhelm.

'Anything but strange, only she isn't a hypocrite. I am fond of her on that account, yes, I am her friend because she represents for me so purely the sex which I have so much reason to hate. I see her as the true Eve, the ancestress of the female sex; that's what they're all like, only they won't admit it.'

Deep in all kinds of conversation, in which Laertes gave vent to his hatred of the female sex in a very lively manner, but without mentioning the cause of this, they had arrived at the wood, which Wilhelm entered in a very upset mood, because Laertes's remarks had rekindled for him the memory of his relationship with Mariane. Not far from the shady spring, beneath magnificent old trees they found Philine sitting alone at a stone table. She sang a merry little song for them as they approached, and when Laertes asked about her companions, she cried out: 'I've led them a fine dance; I've made fools of them, as they deserved. Already on the way here I made a test of their generosity, and when I noticed that they were on the stingy side, I at once made up my mind to punish them. After we had arrived, they asked the waiter what was on the menu, and he reeled off with the usual fluency everything in stock, and more. I saw their embarrassment, they looked at each other, stuttered and asked the price. "Why are you hesitating so long", I exclaimed, "the table is a woman's affair, let me look after it." I then set about ordering a senseless midday-meal, for which a lot of things would have to be fetched from the neighbourhood by messengers. The waiter, whom I had taken into my confidence by pulling wry faces at him, helped me finally, and so we made them so fearful by sketching out a magnificent banquet, that they decided in short to take a walk in the woods, from which it is indeed unlikely that they will return. I've been laughing to myself for a quarter of an hour, and shall go on laughing, as often as I think of their faces.' At table Laertes recalled similar cases; they were soon involved in relating comic stories, and telling of misunderstandings and pranks.

A young man from the town whom they knew came quietly through the woods with a book, sat down with them and praised the fine setting. He drew their attention to the babbling of the spring, the movement of the branches, the patches of light entering from above, and the song of the birds. Philine sang a little song about the cuckoo which the newcomer did not seem to like; he took his leave shortly afterwards.

'If only I didn't have to hear any more about nature and nature scenes,' cried Philine, when he had gone; 'there is nothing more unbearable than to have the pleasure you're enjoying spelt out for you. When the weather's fine, you go walking, just as you dance when the music plays. But whoever wants to think even for a moment about music or about fine weather? It is the dancer, not the violin, who interests us, and it is only too agreeable for a pair of blue eyes to be looking into a pair of beautiful black eyes. What are springs and fountains and rotten old lime trees by comparison!' While speaking thus, she eyed Wilhelm, who was sitting opposite her, with a glance that he could not prevent penetrating at least as far as the antechamber of his heart.

'You are right,' he replied with some embarrassment, 'man is the most interesting thing for man, and perhaps should interest him exclusively. Everything else that surrounds us is either only the element in which we live, or a tool which we use. The more we dwell on it, notice it and become involved in it, the weaker the awareness of our own value and of society becomes. People who lay great value on gardens, buildings, clothes, jewellery or any possession are less sociable and likeable; they lose track of human beings, and only a very few have the gift of pleasing them and bringing them together. Don't we see this also in the theatre? A good actor soon makes us forget a wretched, clumsy décor, whereas the most splendid stage-setting is what makes us really notice the lack of good actors.'

After the meal Philine sat down in a shady spot in the tall grass. Her two friends had to procure for her quantities of flowers. She wound for herself a complete wreath and placed it on her head; she looked unbelievably attractive. There were sufficient flowers for another wreath; she wove this one too, while the two men sat beside her. When it was finished, amid all kinds of jokes and allusions, she placed it on Wilhelm's head with the greatest charm, and moved it more than once into a different position until it seemed to be properly in place. 'And I shall go away empty-handed it seems,' Laertes said.

'Not at all,' rejoined Philine. 'You shall have nothing to complain about.' She took her wreath from her head and placed it on Laertes.

'If we were rivals,' the latter said, 'we should be able to quarrel very fiercely as to which of the two of us you favour more.'

'Then you would be proper fools,' she answered, bending towards him and offering him her mouth to kiss, but at once turning aside, putting her arm round Wilhelm and impressing a lively kiss on his lips. 'Which tastes best?' she asked teasingly.

'Strange!' cried Laertes, 'It seems as if that sort of thing could never taste of wormwood.'

'As little as any gift which someone enjoys without envy and self-will,' said Philine. 'But now I should like to dance for an hour,' she exclaimed, 'and then no doubt we must look to our acrobats again.'

They went home and found music there. Philine, who was a good dancer, enlivened her two companions. Wilhelm was not unskilful, but he lacked trained practice. His two friends undertook to instruct him.

They came late. The acrobats had already started to display their skills. Many spectators had assembled in the square, but as our friends came out, they were aware of a turmoil which had drawn a great number of people to the doorway of the inn where Wilhelm had put up. Wilhelm leapt across to see what it was, and, as he pressed through the throng, he was horrified to see the leader of the company of acrobats endeavouring to drag the strange child by the hair out of the house and beating the little body mercilessly with a whip-handle.

Wilhelm rushed like lightning at the man and seized him by the front. 'Let the child go!' he shouted like a madman, 'or one of us won't leave this place alive.' At the same time he took hold of the fellow by the throat with a strength which only anger can produce, so that the latter thought that he was suffocating, released the child and tried to defend himself against the attacker. Some people who felt pity for the child, but had not dared to begin a dispute, at once seized the acrobat's arms, disarmed him and threatened him with many abusive words. The latter who now saw himself limited only to the weapons of his mouth began to swear and curse horribly: the lazy, useless creature would not do her duty; she was refusing to dance the egg-dance which he had promised the public; he would kill her, and no one was to prevent him. He tried to free himself in order to look for the child who had hidden herself among the crowd. Wilhelm held him back and cried: 'You are not to see or touch this creature again until you have given an account in a court of justice of where you stole her; I shall drive you to the limit; you shan't escape me.' This speech, which Wilhelm had spoken in heat, without thoughts and intent, from dark feeling, or, if you like, from inspiration, quietened the enraged man. He cried: 'Why should I bother with the useless creature! Pay me what her clothes cost me, and you can keep her; let us come to an agreement this very evening.' After that he hurried away to continue the interrupted performance and to assuage the restlessness of the audience by means of some interesting tricks.

Now that it had become quiet, Wilhelm searched for the child, but she was nowhere to be found. Some claimed to have seen her in the attic, others on the roofs of neighbouring houses. After she had been sought everywhere, one had to calm down and wait to see if she would not come along again of her own accord.

Meanwhile Narcissus had gone home, and Wilhelm asked him about the fortunes and origins of the child. Narcissus new nothing of this, for he had not long been with the company, but on the other hand talked about his own adventures with great ease and much frivolity. When Wilhelm congratulated him on the extent of the applause which he enjoyed, he reacted very indifferently. 'We are accustomed to people laughing at us and admiring our arts; but things are not at all improved by the extraordinary applause. The manager pays us, and it's up to him to look after himself.' He took his leave and wished to go away quickly.

In answer to the question as to where he wanted to go so quickly, the young man smiled and admitted that his appearance and gifts attracted to him a more tangible form of applause than that of the public in general. He said he had received messages from some ladies, who were very keenly desirous of getting to know him better, and that he was afraid that he would hardly be finished before midnight with the visits he had to pay. He continued to talk about his adventures with great honesty, and would have informed him of names, streets and houses, had not Wilhelm rejected such an indiscretion and politely dismissed him.

Meanwhile Laertes had been conversing with Landrinette, and he maintained that she was fully worthy to be a woman and to remain one.

Now the negotiations with the manager about the child took place, and she was made over to our friend for thirty Taler, for which sum the black-bearded, ferocious Italian completely ceded his claims; he was unwilling to say anything more about the origins of the child than that he had been looking after her since the death of his brother, who had been called 'the big devil' because of his extraordinary skill.

The next morning was mostly spent in searching for the child. They searched in vain all corners of the house and neighbourhood; she had disappeared, and it was feared that she might have jumped into some water or harmed herself in some other way.

Philine's charms could not deflect our friend's unrest. He spent a sad, reflective day. Even in the evening, when acrobats and dancers were deploying all their resources in order to please the public, his feelings could not be cheered or distracted.

The influx from neighbouring localities had increased the number of people to an unusual degree and so the snowball of applause also swelled to an enormous size. The leap over the daggers and through the barrel with paper bases caused a great sensation. The strong man, to general horror, terror and surprise, lay with his head and feet on a couple of chairs that had been pushed apart, and allowed an anvil to be lifted on to his unsupported body and a horseshoe to be forged on it by some journeyman-blacksmiths.

The so-called human pyramid, where a row of men, standing on the shoulders of a first row, again carries women and youngsters, so that finally a living pyramid emerges whose tip is adorned by a child, standing on its head, as knob and weathervane, had also never previously been seen in this region, and it brought the whole performance to a dignified conclusion. Narcissus and Landrinette allowed themselves to be carried in sedan chairs on the shoulders of the others through the best streets of the town amidst loud shouts of joy from the people. Ribbons, bunches of flowers and silk kerchieves were thrown at them, and people pressed close to see them in the face. Everyone seemed happy to be looking at them and to be deemed worthy of receiving a glance from them.

'What actor, what writer, indeed what human being generally would not regard himself as being at the pinnacle of his ambitions, if he evoked a general response of this nature through some noble word or a good deed? What a fine sentiment it would surely be, if one could disseminate good, noble, humane feelings equally quickly through an electric shock, and could arouse such delight among the people as these persons have done through their physical skill; if one could give to the crowd a sympathy for all that relates to the human condition, if one could arouse and move them by the enactment of happiness and unhappiness, wisdom and folly, even nonsense and silliness, and could bring to their stagnating selves free, vital and pure movement!' These were our friend's words, and as neither Philine nor Laertes seemed in the mood for continuing such a discussion, he entertained himself with these favourite considerations of his, as he took a walk round the town late at night, once more pursuing with all the liveliness and freedom of an unrestricted imagination his old wish to present in tangible form by means of drama the good, the noble and the great.

Chapter Five

Next day, when the acrobats had departed with great clamour, Mignon immediately appeared again and came along while Wilhelm and Laertes were continuing their fencing exercises in the ante-room. 'Where've you been?' Wilhelm asked in a friendly way; 'we've been worried about you.' The child did not answer, and looked at him. 'You're ours now,' cried Laertes, 'we've bought you.'—'What did you pay?' the child asked drily.—'A hundred ducats,' replied Laertes; 'if you give them back, you can be free.' —'That's a lot, I suppose?' the child asked.—'Oh yes, just you behave properly.'—'I will be your servant,' she replied.

From that moment on she observed exactly what sort of services the waiter had to perform for the two friends, and already on the next day she was no longer willing for him to come into the room. She wanted to do everything herself, and performed her tasks, admittedly slowly and at times clumsily, yet precisely and with great care.

She would often stand by a vessel with water and wash her face with such great diligence and vehemence that she almost rubbed her cheeks sore, until Laertes learnt from her by questioning and teasing that she was attempting by all means to get rid of the make-up from her cheeks and that in her zeal at doing this she considered the redness which she had caused by the rubbing to be the most recalcitrant make-up. They spoke to her, and she desisted, and after she had regained composure, her complexion was revealed as a beautiful brown, though heightened with just a little red.

Attracted by the wanton charms of Philine and by the mysterious presence of the child more than he would admit to himself, Wilhelm spent a number of days in this strange company and justified it in his own eyes by assiduous practice in fencing and dancing, believing that he would not easily find the opportunity for this again.

He was not a little surprised and to a certain extent pleased when one day he saw Mr. and Mrs. Melina arrive who, immediately after the first cheerful greeting, inquired after the manageress and the rest of the actors, and learnt with great alarm that the former had gone off a long time ago and that the actors had dispersed, apart from a few.

The young couple had looked for engagements at various places after their union in the accomplishment of which, as we know, Wilhelm had been of assistance, but had not found any work and had finally been directed to this little town, where several persons whom they had met on their travels would have liked to see a good theatre.

Philine was not at all pleased about Mrs. Melina, nor the vivacious Laertes about Mr. Melina, when they became acquainted. They at once wanted to be rid of the newcomers, and Wilhelm could not persuade them to a favourable opinion, although he repeatedly assured them that these were really good people.

Actually the gay life that our three adventurers had been leading hitherto had been upset in more than one way by the expansion of the group; for Melina began at once to haggle and wrangle in the inn (he had found accommodation in the one where Philine was staying). He wanted better quarters, ampler meals and prompter service for little money. It was not long before innkeeper and waiter were looking annoyed, and if the others, in order to live cheerfully, put up with everything and just paid quickly, in order not to have to think any longer about what had already been consumed, the meal whose bill Melina regularly settled straightaway had to be gone through every time from the beginning again, so that Philine described him without ceremony as an animal chewing the cud.

Madame Melina was even more unpopular with the cheery girl. This young lady was not without education, but she was quite lacking in mind and spirit. She was not bad at declaiming, and she always wanted to do this; however, it was soon noticeable that it was only a declamation of words which weighed heavily on individual parts and failed to express the feeling of the whole. With all this it was not easy for anyone, in particular men, to find her unpleasant. On the contrary, those who kept her company usually ascribed to her a fine understanding; for she was what I would like to call in a few words a woman capable of adapting herself to and conforming with the expectation of others; she knew how to flatter a friend, about whose respect for her she was concerned, with particular attention, to follow his ideas as long as possible, but as soon as they were completely beyond her horizons, to take up ecstatically some new phenomenon. She understood when to speak and when to be silent, and although she was not malicious she knew how to be on the look-out with great caution for the other person's weak spot.

Chapter Six

In the meantime Melina had been making detailed inquiries about the remains of the previous company. Scenery as well as wardrobe material had been made over to some dealers, and a notary had received instructions from the manageress that he could agree, using his own initiative, to its sale under certain conditions, if buyers could be found. Melina wanted to see the things, and took Wilhelm with him. When the storerooms were opened, the latter felt a certain attraction towards all this which, however, he did not admit to himself. Although the blotchy scenery was in bad condition, and although Turkish and heathen costumes, old caricature-coats for men and women, and cowls for magicians, Jews and priests were hardly prepossessing, he could not resist the feeling that he had found the happiest moments of his life in the presence of comparable lumber. If Melina had been able to look into his heart, he would have pressed him more zealously to provide a sum of money for the liberation, reconstruction and revitalization of these dispersed articles. 'What a happy man I could be', exclaimed Melina, 'if I only possessed two hundred Taler in order, as a start, to get possession of these first theatrical requisites. How quickly I would put a little play together that would certainly support us at once in this town and district.' Wilhelm was silent, and both were thoughtful as they left the treasures that were again locked away.

From this time onward Melina talked of nothing apart from plans and proposals as to how a theatre could be set up and at the same time how a profit could be made from it. He tried to interest Philine and Laertes, and suggestions were put to Wilhelm that he should advance money and take up securities. But it was not until this subject was raised that it properly occurred to the latter that he should not have stayed here so long; he conveyed his apologies and wanted to make preparations to continue on his journey.

Mignon's appearance and character had in the meantime become ever more attractive to him. There was something strange about the child in all her comings and goings. She did not go up or down the stairs, but leapt; she climbed up the corridor bannisters, and before you knew where you were, she was sitting high up on the wardrobe where she would stay quiet for a while. Wilhelm had also noticed that she had a particular way of greeting. For some time now she had been greeting him with her arms across her breast. On many days she was wholly mute, while at other times gave more answers to various questions, always in a strange fashion, and in such a way that it was not possible to distinguish wit from ignorance of the language, for she spoke broken German interspersed with French and Italian. In her serving activities the child was indefatigable, getting up early with the sunrise; she retired in good time, however, in the evening, slept in an attic on the bare floor and could not be persuaded to accept a bed or a straw mattress. He often found her washing herself. Her clothes were kept clean too, although everything had been mended two or three times over. Wilhelm was also told that she went to mass very early each morning, and he followed her once, and saw her kneeling with her rosary in a corner of the church, praying devoutly. She did not notice him; he went home, thought a lot about this creature, and could not come to any definite conclusion about her.

More pressure from Melina concerning a sum of money needed for redeeming the above-mentioned theatre requisites persuaded Wilhelm even more to think of his departure. He wished to write on that very mail-day to his family, who had heard nothing from him for a long time; what is more, he really did begin a letter to Werner, and had already got some way in the account of his adventures, in which process, without noticing it himself, he had strayed several times from the truth, when to his annoyance he found on the other side of the piece of paper lines of poetry already written which he had started to copy out from his writing-tablet for Madame Melina. With some annoyance he tore up the sheet of paper and deferred the repetition of his confession until the next mail-day.

Chapter Seven

Our company was once more together, and Philine, who was exceedingly attentive about each horse that passed and each carriage that came by, shouted out with great vivacity: 'Our Pedant! There goes our darling Pedant! Whoever has he got with him!' She called and waved out of the window, and the carriage stopped.

A wretchedly poor devil who, to judge from his threadbare, greyish-brown coat and his badly kept undergarments, could have been taken for a tutor of the type that moulder in academic institutions, stepped out of the carriage and, as he raised his hat to greet Philine, revealed a badly powdered, but incidentally very stiff wig, and Philine threw him many kisses.

Just as she found her happiness in loving some men and enjoying their love, so she also took no less pleasure in making fun in a very flippant way of the rest whom she did not love at the moment.

In the noise with which she received this old friend they forgot to pay attention to the others who followed after him. But Wilhelm believed he recognized the two women and an oldish man who came with them. It also transpired soon that he had seen all three of them several times some years ago with the troupe that used to play in his home town. The daughters had grown since that time; but the old man had changed little. He usually played the parts of good-hearted, blustering old men, of whom the German theatre is not short, and who are also not infrequently to be met in everyday life. For as it belongs to the character of our compatriots to do good without show, they do not often think that there is also a way of doing what is right with elegance and charm, and, driven by a spirit of contradiction, they then easily make the mistake of displaying through disagreeable behaviour their dearest virtue in reverse.

Our actor played such roles very well, and he played them so often and exclusively that in the process he had assumed a similar way of behaving in ordinary life.

Wilhelm became very agitated as soon as he recognized him, for he remembered how often he had seen this man on the stage by the side of his beloved Mariane; he could still hear his scolding and the coaxing voice with which she had to respond to his rough manner in many roles.

The first, lively question to the newcomers, whether work could be found and hoped for away from the town, was regrettably answered in the negative, and the questioners had to hear that the theatre companies where they had made inquiries were full up and that some of them were indeed anxious in case they might have to scatter because of the impending war. The Blustering Old Man, with his daughters, had given up an advantageous engagement out of chagrin as well as out of love of change, and had hired a coach together with the Pedant, whom he met on the journey, in order to come here, where they also found that the situation was critical.

Wilhelm was very thoughtful during the time when the others were talking in a very lively way about their own affairs. He wanted to speak to the old man on his own, wished to hear about

Mariane, at the same time was afraid to do so, and was in a state of greatest agitation.

The agreeable qualities of the newly arrived ladies could not snatch him from his dream; but an altercation that arose made him pay attention. Friedrich, the blonde-haired boy who usually waited on Philine, was resisting energetically this time, when he was supposed to lay the table and bring along the food. 'I have undertaken to serve you', he said, 'But not to wait on everybody.' They became involved in a fierce dispute about this. Philine insisted that he had his duties to carry out, and when he resisted obstinately, she told him unceremoniously that he could go off wherever he wanted to.

'Do you think, for instance, that I can't be separated from you?' he called out, went obstinately away, tied up his bundle and at once hurried out of the house. 'Mignon, go and get us what we need,' said Philine; 'tell the waiter and give a hand with the waiting!'

Mignon went up to Wilhelm and asked in her laconic way: 'Shall I? May I?' And Wilhelm replied: 'My child, do what Mademoiselle tells you.'

The child took care of everything and waited on the guests the whole evening with great care. After the meal Wilhelm tried to go for a walk alone with the old man; he succeeded, and after various questions about how things had gone with him so far, the conversation turned to the former theatre company, and Wilhelm at last ventured to ask about Mariane.

'Don't talk to me about that dreadful creature!' the old man cried; 'I have sworn not to think of her any more.' Wilhelm was startled at this comment, but was in even greater embarrassment when the old man continued to rail at her frivolity and dissoluteness. How glad our friend would have been to have cut off the conversation; but now he had to put up with the blustering effusions of this strange man.

'I am ashamed that I was so fond of her,' the latter continued. 'But if you had known the girl at all closely, you would be sure to excuse me. She was so agreeable, natural and good, so obliging and in every way acceptable. I should never have imagined that impertinence and ingratitude would be the main features of her character.'

Wilhelm had already prepared himself to hear the worst about her, when with surprise he noticed all at once that the old man's tone of voice became milder, his flow of words finally came to a stop and he took a handkerchief out of his pocket in order to dry the tears which in the end interrupted his speech.

'What is it?' exclaimed Wilhelm. 'What causes your feelings all at once to take on so contrary a direction? Don't hide it from me; I take more interest in the fate of this girl than you believe; only do tell me everything.'

'I've little to say,' the old man replied, reverting again to his serious, irritable manner; 'I shall never forgive her for what I have put up with for her sake. She always had a certain trust in me,' he went on; 'I loved her like a daughter, and while my wife was still alive, I had decided to look after her and rescue her from the clutches of the old woman from whose guidance I did not promise myself much that was good. My wife died, the plan collapsed.

'Towards the end of our stay in your home town, it's not three years ago, I noticed that she looked distinctly sad; I asked her, but she avoided replying. In the end we started on our travels. She went with me in the coach, and I noticed, and she also soon admitted it, that she was pregnant and that she was in a state of greatest anxiety, in case our manager should dismiss her. What is more, it wasn't long before he made the discovery, at once terminated her contract, which in any case was only on a six-week basis, paid what was owing to her, and, ignoring all representations, left her behind in a poor inn in a small town.

'The devil take all dissolute whores!' the old man cried out with anger, 'and particularly this one who has ruined so many hours of my life. Why should I go on at length about how I took interest in her, what I did for her and gave to her, and how I cared for her, even at a distance. I would rather throw my money into a pond and spend my time training mangy dogs than ever again pay the slightest attention to such a creature. What was it? At first I received letters of thanks, news about some of the places where she was staying, and finally not a word more, not even thanks for the money that I had sent her for her confinement. Oh, the dissimulation and frivolity of women go so well together that they provide them with a comfortable life and cause an honest fellow many an hour of vexation!'

Chapter Eight

One can imagine Wilhelm's state of mind when he came home after this conversation. All his old wounds had been re-opened, and the feeling that she had not been wholly unworthy of his love had come to life again; for in the old man's interest, in the praise that he had to bestow on her in spite of himself, her full amiability had been shown to our friend again; indeed, even the vehement man's forceful indictment contained nothing that could diminish her in Wilhelm's eyes. For the latter confessed himself to be an accomplice in her offences, and her silence finally did not seem to him culpable; he rather only had melancholy thoughts about this, and saw her straying about the world without help as a woman in childbed and as a mother, presumably with his own child, ideas which aroused in him most painful feelings.

Mignon had been waiting for him and held a light for him as he went upstairs. When she had put down the light, she asked him to permit her to perform one of her turns for him that evening. He would have preferred to refuse this, especially as he did not know what was involved. But there was nothing he could refuse this good creature. After a short time she came in again. She had a carpet under her arm, which she unfolded on the ground. Wilhelm let her proceed. She then brought four lights, placing one on each tip of the rug. A little basket with eggs, which she then fetched, made her intention clearer. She now stepped this way and that in artful, measured steps, and placed the eggs apart from each other at certain distances; then she called someone in who waited at the house and played the violin. He went into the corner with his instrument; she blindfolded her eyes, gave a sign and began her movements at the same time as the music, like wound-up clockwork, while accompanying time and melody with the beating of castanets.

She danced with agility, lightness, speed and precision. She stepped so sharply and surely between the eggs and down by them that with every moment the thought came to mind that she would have to trample on the one of them or else hurl another away in the course of her movements. Not at all! She touched none of them, although she wound her way through the rows with all kinds of steps, both narrow and wide, indeed even with leaps and finally half-kneeling.

She took her course without stopping, like a piece of clockwork, and the strange music gave a new impulse to the dance as it continually started again at the beginning and whirled on its way at each repetition. Wilhelm was quite absorbed by the strange spectacle; he forgot his cares, followed every moment of the beloved creature, and wondered how excellently her character developed in this dance.

She showed herself as severe, sharp, dry, forcible and, in gentle postures, solemn rather than agreeable. At this moment he felt all at once what he had already been sensible of on Mignon's behalf. He longed to take this forlorn being to his heart in place of a child, to feel her in his arms and with a father's love to arouse in her an enjoyment of life.

The dance came to an end; she quietly rolled the eggs into a heap with her feet, left none behind, did not damage any and took up her stand, taking the bandage from her eyes and concluding her act with a bow.

Wilhelm thanked her for performing so neatly and so unexpectedly the dance which he had wished to see. He stroked her and regretted that she had taken such great pains over it. He promised her a new dress, to which she replied impulsively: 'Your colour!' This too he promised her, although he did not know clearly what she meant by this. She collected the eggs, placing the rug under her arm, asked if he had any other orders, and bounded out of the door.

He learnt from the musician that for some time she had been taking a lot of trouble to sing to him the dance, which was the well-known fandango, until he was able to play it. Also, the musician said, she had offered him some money, which, however, he had refused to take, for his efforts.

Chapter Nine

After an unquiet night, which our friend spent partly awake and partly frightened in difficult dreams in which he saw Mariane now in all her beauty, now in a wretched state, at one time with a child in her arms, at another time deprived of the infant, morning had scarcely arrived when Mignon already came in with a tailor. She brought with her grey cloth and blue taffeta, and declared in her characteristic way that she would like to have a new little waistcoat and sailor's trousers, with blue lapels and ribbons, of a style comparable to what she had seen on boys in the town.

Since the loss of Mariane Wilhelm had put aside all bright colours. He had got used to grey, the garb of the shades, and only something like a sky-blue lining or a little collar of this colour enlivened that subdued costume to some extent. Eager to be wearing Wilhelm's colours, Mignon urged on the tailor who promised to deliver the work shortly.

The dancing and fencing lessons which our friend took with Laertes were none too successful that day. Furthermore, they were soon interrupted by the arrival of Melina who pointed out at length how by this time a little company had been formed, with which it would already be possible to perform enough plays. He renewed his request that Wilhelm should advance some money for the business, but the latter again displayed his indecision.

With laughter and noise Philine and the girls came in soon after. They had again been thinking up an excursion; for a change of scene and surroundings was a pleasure for which they always longed. To have a meal at a different place every day was their greatest wish. This time it was to be a trip on the water.

The ship, in which they wanted to sail down the pleasant, winding river, had already been booked by the Pedant. Philine was urging people on, the group did not hesitate and were soon on board.

'What shall we do now?' Philine said, afer everyone had seated themselves on the benches.

'The quickest thing to do,' replied Laertes, 'would be for us to extemporize a play. Let everyone take a part which suits his character best, and we will see what success we have.'

'Excellent!' said Wilhelm, 'for in a group where there is no dissembling, where each person follows his own inclination, charm and contentment will not remain for long, and where people are always dissembling, they do not come at all. Therefore, it's not a bad idea to assume the pretence right away and then to be as honest as we like beneath the mask.'

'Yes,' said Laertes, 'that's why it is so pleasant to be with women, for they never let themselves be seen in their natural guise.'

Madame Melina replied: 'That's because they are not so vain as men, who imagine that they are still as charming as they were when nature brought them into being.'

In the meantime they had been journeying between pleasant bushes and hills, between gardens and vineyards, and the young ladies, in particular Madame Melina, expressed their delight at the scenery. Madame Melina even began to recite in solemn tones an agreeable poem of the descriptive type about a similar natural scene; but Philine interrupted her and proposed as a rule that no one should venture to talk about an inanimate object; she vigorously carried through, on the contrary, the proposal of an extempore comedy. The Blustering Old Man was to represent a pensioned-off officer, Laertes an itinerant, unemployed fencing-instructor, the Pedant a Jew, she herself would take on the part of a Tyrolese woman, and she left it to the others to choose their own parts. They were to imagine that they were a group of people who were strangers to one another and who had just come together on a trading ship.

She at once began to play her part along with the Jew, and there was a mood of general cheerfulness.

They had not been travelling for long before the boatman stopped in order to take on board, with the permission of the assembled company, a further person who was standing at the bank and who had been waving.

'That's just what we needed,' cried Philine; 'as yet the group of voyagers has not had a stowaway.'

An imposing man got into the boat, and from his clothing and his venerable appearance he might well have been taken for a clergyman. He greeted the company, and they thanked him in their ways and soon introduced him to the game they were playing. Thereupon he took the part of a country clergyman, and to the astonishment of everybody played the part in the most skilful way, at one time admonishing, at another telling little stories, allowing a few weak sides to be seen and yet knowing how to receive continued respect.

Meanwhile, everyone who fell out of his role one single time had to pay a forfeit. Philine had been collecting these with great care and had threatened the clergyman in particular with many kisses the next time the score was being reckoned, although he never was penalized. Melina, on the other hand, was completely deprived, shirt buttons and buckles and everything on his person that was movable had been taken from him by Philine; for he was trying to depict an Englishman on his travels and could not get into the part in any sort of way.

Time passed in the pleasantest way, however, each person had been exercising his imagination and wit as much as possible, and each one had furbished his role with agreeable and entertaining jokes. In this manner they came to the locality where they wished to spend the day, and while they were walking Wilhelm soon got into an interesting conversation with the clergyman, as we shall call him on account of his appearance and the part he had been playing.

'I find that this kind of exercise is very useful among actors, indeed, in a group of friends and acquaintances,' the stranger said. 'It is the best way of taking people out of themselves and then leading them back to themselves by means of a détour. The usage should be introduced in every troupe of actors, so that they would have to practice this type of exercise a good number of times, and the public would certainly be the beneficiaries, if once a month an unwritten play could be performed, though certainly the actors would have had to prepare themselves in several rehearsals.'

'One should not think of an extempore play as one that would be created immediately, on the spur of the moment,' Wilhelm replied, 'but as one where indeed the plan, the action and the division into scenes would be fixed, though the execution would be left to the actor.'

'Quite right,' the stranger said, 'and particularly as regards the execution, a play of this sort would gain an extraordinary amount, as soon as the actors had once got going. Not execution by means of words, for the deliberating writer indeed has to adorn his work with these, but execution through gestures and facial expressions, exclamations and what goes with them, in short, mute, half-articulated acting, which gradually seems to be getting quite lost among our people. It is true, there are actors in Germany whose body shows what they think and feel, and who know how to anticipate a speech with delicate, graceful body movements and how to link the pauses in a dialogue with the whole by means of agreeable miming; but a form of exercise which would be of assistance to a felicitous natural gift and would enable this latter to vie with the writer is not practised as sufficiently as might be desirable for the comfort of those who visit the theatre.'

'But should not a felicitous natural gift be the first and last thing that alone would bring an actor, like every other type of artist, indeed, like every type of person perhaps, to so high an ambition?', Wilhelm rejoined.

'It might well be the first thing and the last thing, the beginning and the end; but in between there could be a lot lacking in the artist, unless education in the first place makes him into what he is intended to be, and what is more, education at the early stages; for perhaps the man to whom genius is ascribed is in a worse way than someone who possesses only ordinary capabilities; for the former can more easily be badly educated and more abruptly urged along false paths than the latter.'

'But will not genius save itself,' replied Wilhelm, 'and itself heal the wounds that it has inflicted on itself?'

'Not at all,' the other answered, 'or at least only in a makeshift manner; for nobody should believe that they can get over first childhood impressions. If someone has grown up in commendable freedom, surrounded by beautiful and noble objects, in the company of good people, if his masters have taught him the things he had to learn first, in order that the rest might be understood the more easily, if what he has learnt he never needs to unlearn, if his first actions were so directed that he can in future do good more easily and more conveniently, without his having to break himself of anything, this person will lead a purer, more perfect and happier life than someone who has misplaced the first energies of his youth in opposition and error. There is so much said and written about education, and I see only a few people who can grasp the simple but great idea that includes all else in itself, and put this into execution.'

'That may well be true,' said Wilhelm, 'for every person is limited enough to wish to bring up the other man as a model of himself. How happy, therefore, are those in whom fate, which educates everyone in its own fashion, takes an interest!'

'Fate is an elegant but expensive tutor,' the other replied with a smile. 'I would always rather rely on a human master's power of reason. Fate, for whose wisdom I have every respect, may well have a very clumsy mouthpiece in chance, through which it works. For it is seldom that chance appears to carry out in a precise and pure manner what fate has decreed.'

'You seem to be uttering a very strange thought,' Wilhelm rejoined.

'Not at all! Most things we meet with in life justify my opinion. Do not many undertakings show great significance in the first place, and do not most of them peter out in something trivial?'

'You're joking.'

'And isn't it the same in the case of what happens to individual persons?' the other continued. 'Supposing that fate had destined someone to be a good actor (and why should not fate also provide us with good actors?), but unfortunately chance led the young man to a puppet theatre, where in his youth he could not restrain himself from participating in something tasteless, from finding something silly tolerable, even interesting, and thus receiving in a wrong way those youthful impressions which never disappear and from which we can never remove a certain attachment.'

'What makes you mention the puppet-theatre?' Wilhelm interpolated with some consternation.

'It was only an arbitrary example; if you don't like it, we will take another. Supposing that fate had destined someone to be a great painter and it pleased chance to banish him in his youth to dirty hovels, stables and barns—do you believe that such a man would ever raise himself up to purity, nobility, and freedom of spirit? The more eagerly he has in his youth grasped hold of the impure element and in his own way idealized it, the more forcibly will it avenge itself on him in his later life, since it will have bound itself to him in the closest manner, though meanwhile he has been attempting to repudiate it. He who has spent his early life in bad, insignificant society will, even if later he can have something better, always look back with longing to that society, whose impression will have remained with him along with the memory of youthful joys which can seldom be renewed.'

It can be imagined that the rest of the company gradually went off in the course of this conversation. Philine in particular had stepped aside rightaway from the start. They came back to the others by a side-path. Philine brought out the forfeits which had to be redeemed in all sorts of ways, in the course of which the stranger endeared himself very much to the whole company and especially to the ladies by means of the neatest devices and through his informal participation; and so the hours of the day took their course in the pleasantest way amid jokes, kisses and all kinds of banter.

Chapter Ten

When they wanted to go back home again, they looked around for their clergyman; but he had disappeared and was nowhere to be found.

'It isn't civil of the man, who otherwise seems to be very well-mannered,' Madame Melina said, 'to leave a group of people that have received him in such a friendly way, without saying goodbye.'

'I've been thinking the whole time where I might have seen this strange man before,' said Laertes. 'I was just going to ask him about it on taking leave.'

'It was the same as far as I was concerned,' rejoined Wilhelm, 'and I certainly would not have let him go until he had told us something more about himself. Unless I am very much mistaken, I must have talked to him already somewhere before.'

'And yet you could really be wrong here,' Philine said. 'This man in fact only has the deceptive appearance of an acqaintance because he looks like a human being and not like any Tom, Dick or Harry.'

'What's that supposed to mean,' said Laertes, 'don't we look like human beings as well?'

'I know what I'm talking about,' replied Philine 'and if you don't understand me, never mind. I'm surely not supposed to give an interpretation of my own words.'

Two coaches drove up. There was praise for the forethought of Laertes, who had ordered them. Philine took a seat by the side of Madame Melina opposite to Wilhelm, and the others fitted in as best they could. Laertes himself rode back to the town on Wilhelm's horse which had also made the journey out.

Philine had scarcely got into the carriage before she began to sing pleasant songs and to turn the conversation to stories, which, she maintained, could successfully be offered in dramatic form. By this clever turn to the conversation she had soon put her young friend into the best of spirits, and from the wealth of his living storehouse of images, he at once constructed an entire play with all its acts, scenes, characters and complexities. It was thought a good idea to intersperse some arias and songs; these were composed, and Philine, who entered into everything, straightaway fitted popular melodies to them and sang them impromptu.

It so happened that today was her good day, her very good day; she was able to enliven our friend with all kinds of teasing; he felt happy in a way that he had not for along time.

Since that terrible discovery had torn him from Mariane's side, he had remained faithful to the vow to be cautious in face of the engulfing trap of a female embrace, to steer clear of the faithless sex, and to lock up within his bosom his griefs, his inclinations, and his sweet desires. The conscientiousness with which he observed this oath gave his whole being a secret nourishment, and as his heart could not stay without expressing itself, a form of affectionate communication now became a need for him. He again went around as if accompanied by the first youthful aura of enthusiasm, his eyes apprehended joyfully every charming subject, and never had his judgment about a charming person been more considerate. How dangerous the bold girl inevitably was for him in such a position can unfortunately be realized only too well.

At home in Wilhelm's room they found everything already prepared for their reception, the chairs put ready for a reading and placed in the middle, the table upon which the punchbowl was to be set.

The German plays about medieval knights were just new at that time, and had attracted the attention and favour of the public. The old Pedant had brought along one of this sort of play, and they decided to read it together. They sat down. Wilhelm got hold of the copy and started to read.

The knights in armour, the old castles, the frankness, integrity and honesty, but especially the independence, of the characters were received with great applause. Wilhelm as reader did his best, and the group were quite beside themselves. Between the second and third acts the punch came in a big bowl; and as there was a lot of drinking and clinking of glasses in the play itself, nothing was more natural than that the company each time put themselves in the place of the heroes, clinked their glasses and proposed toasts to the favourites among the characters.

Everyone was enflamed by the fire of the noblest national spirit. How pleased this company of Germans was to enjoy themselves in poetic style in accordance with their own character on their very own ground! A quite unbelievable effect was produced especially by the vaults and cellars, the ruined castle, the moss and the hollow trees, but above all by gipsy scenes at night and the secret court of justice. Each actor now saw himself soon displaying his German qualities before the public in helmet and armour, each actress now saw herself likewise displaying these qualities by means of a big, stand-up collar. Each one wanted to take possession straightaway of a name from the play or from German history, and Madame Melina averred that the son or daughter she was expecting should be baptized none other than Adalbert or Mechthilde.

Towards the fifth act the applause became noisier and louder, indeed finally, when the hero really escaped from his oppressor and the tyrant was punished, the rapture was so great that they vowed they had never spent such happy hours. Melina, enthused by drink, was the loudest of them, and as the second punchbowl was emptied and midnight was drawing near, Laertes swore solemnly that nobody was sufficiently deserving ever to place his lips on these glasses again, and with this assertion he hurled his glass behind him and through the window-panes into the street. The others followed his example, and in spite of the protestations of the innkeeper who came hastening along, the punchbowl itself, which after such a party should never again be profaned through unholy drink, was broken into a thousand pieces. Philine, whose drunkenness showed least, although the two girls were lying on the settee not in the most decent of postures, egged on the others with malicious pleasure to be noisy. Madame Melina was reciting some high-flown poems, and her husband, who was not very pleasant in drink, began to complain about the bad preparation of the punch, asserted that he knew how to organize a party very differently, and when Laertes told him to be quiet he became ever cruder and louder, so that Laertes, without much further hesitation threw the fragments of the bowl at his head and thus increased the noise not a little.

Meanwhile the patrol had arrived and demanded to be let into the house. Wilhelm, very heated with his reading, although he had not drunk much, had his hands full with pacifying the people with the support of the innkeeper by means of money and soothing words and to direct the members of the company on their way home in their dubious condition. When he came back, he was overcome by sleep and threw himself in ill humour on to the bed without getting undressed, and nothing was comparable to the unpleasant feeling he had when he opened his eyes the next morning and looked with dismay at the devastations of the day before, at the rubbish and the bad after-effects which an intelligent, lively and well-intentioned work of literature had occasioned.

Chapter Eleven

After short reflection he at once summoned the innkeeper and asked for the cost of the damages and of the bill to be charged to his account. At the same time he learnt, not without annoyance, that his horse had been handled yesterday by Laertes, as he was riding into the town, in such a way that it had become lame, as one might say, and that the smith held out little hope of its recovery.

A greeting from Philine, which she waved to him from her window, put him again into a cheerful mood, however, and he at once went into the nearest shop in order to buy her a small present, which he still owed her in return for the powder knife, and we have to confess that he did not restrict himself in the limits of a return present of a proportionate kind. He not only bought her a pair of very pretty ear-rings, but also took another hat and scarf and some other trifles, which he had seen her throw away in a spendthrift manner on the first day.

Madame Melina, who observed him just as he was handing over his gifts, sought an opportunity already before the meal time to speak to him very seriously about his feeling for this girl, and he was all the more astonished as he thought he merited anything but these reproofs. He swore solemnly that it had by no means entered his mind to turn to this person, whose whole mode of life was well known to him; he apologized as best he could for his friendly and well-mannered behaviour towards her, but in no way satisfied Madame Melina; rather she became more and more irritated as she could not but notice that flattery, by means of which she had acquired a sort of inclination from our friend, was not enough to defend this possession against the attacks of a lively, younger person who was also more happily endowed by nature.

When they came to the dining table they found that her husband was likewise in a very bad humour, and he was already starting to vent his mood on trivialities when the innkeeper came in and announced a harpist. 'You will certainly find pleasure in the music and the songs of this man, he said; no one who hears him can refrain from admiring him and passing some little thing on to him.'

'Send him away,' replied Melina. 'The last thing I want to do now is to hear an organ-grinder, and in any case we've got singers among ourselves who would be glad to earn something.' He accompanied these words with a malicious side-glance at Philine. She understood him, and to his annoyance was immediately ready to give protection to the singer who had been announced. She turned to Wilhelm and said, 'What about hearing the man? Are we to do nothing to save ourselves from wretched boredom?'

Melina wanted to answer her, and the quarrel would have become more spirited, if Wilhelm had not greeted the man as he entered at that moment and beckoned him to come over.

The figure of this strange guest took the whole company by surprise, and he had already taken possession of a chair before anyone had the heart to question him or to say anything else. His bald crown was fringed by a little grey hair, big blue eyes glanced gently beneath long white eyebrows. A long white beard was attached to a well-formed nose without concealing the pleasing lip, and a long dark-brown robe enveloped the slim body from head to foot; and so he began to preludize on the harp which he had placed in front of him.

The pleasant sounds which he enticed from the instrument quite soon cheered the company.

'You are accustomed to singing, good old man,' Philine said.

'Give us something that will delight heart and mind at the same time as the senses,' said Wilhelm. 'The instrument should only accompany the voice; for melodies, passages and runs without word and meaning seem to me to be like butterflies or beautiful, gaily-coloured birds which soar in the air before our eyes, and which in any event we should like to seize and appropriate;

whereas song rises to heaven like a guardian spirit and arouses the better self within us to accompany it.'

The old man looked at Wilhelm, then looked upwards, played a few notes on the harp and began his song. It contained a praise of singing, celebrated the good fortune of singers and exhorted people to honour them. He performed the song with so much life and truthfulness that it seemed as if he had composed it at this moment and for this occasion. Wilhelm could scarcely restrain himself from embracing him; only the fear of provoking loud laughter held him back on his chair; for the others were already making some silly remarks in an undertone and were arguing as to whether the man was a priest or a Jew.

When they asked who was the author of the song, he did not give a definite answer; he only assured them that he was plentifully provided with songs and that all he wished was to give pleasure. In general the company was cheerful and happy, indeed even Melina was quite forthcoming in his way, and while they were chatting and joking among themselves the old man began in the cleverest fashion to sing the praise of sociable living. He praised unity and obligingness with ingratiating tones. Suddenly the singing became dry, rough and intricate as he deplored spiteful taciturnity, narrow-minded hostility and dangerous dissension, and everyone was glad to discard these uncomfortable fetters when, borne on the wings of an urgent melody, he commended peacemakers and sang of the happiness of those who find each other again.

He had scarcely finished when Wilhelm called to him: 'Whoever you may be, coming in our midst as a helpful guardian spirit with a voice that brings blessing and animation, receive my respect and gratitude! Feel how we all admire you, and trust us if there is anything you need!'

The old man was silent, first let his fingers slip over the strings, then he attacked them more boldly and sang:

'Upon the bridge and beyond the gate,
What are the sounds I hear?
Oh, let the hall reverberate
With melody for our ear.'
The king had spoken, the page-boy fled;
The lad came back, the king then said:
'Let's have the old man with us.'

'To you be greetings, lords afar,
Fair ladies, greetings too!
How rich a sky, with star on star!

Who could give names to you?
In this splendid, wondrous hall
Be closed, my eyes; there's no time at all
To stare with surprise and pleasure.'

And as the minstrel shut his eyes
Full harmonies were heard:
The glance of the knight could boldly rise,
The lady's hardly stirred.
The minstrel's song had pleased the king
Who, recompensing him, did bring
The gift of a golden chain.

'Oh give me not the chain of gold,
The chain is for the knights,
Before whose faces bold
Foes' lances split in fights.
Or let your chancellor have the fate
Of bearing now the golden weight
Along with other burdens.

'I sing as the bird sings up on high
Amidst the leaves and boughs.
The heartfelt song that comes as a cry
Its own reward allows;
But if I may, one thing I request;
A drink of wine, of the very best,
Brought in a crystal glass.'

He raised the glass and drank the wine:
'Oh, drink refreshing swift!
Oh, three times blessed are house and line
Where such is a tiny gift!
If things go well with you, give thought
To me, who thank you for what you have brought,
And give your thanks to God.'

When, after finishing the song, the singer took up a glass of wine that had been poured out for him and with a friendly expression drained it, while turning towards his benefactors, a general cheerfulness arose in the company. They clapped and called to him, wishing that this glass of wine would contribute to his health and to the strengthening of his old limbs. He sang some further ballads and aroused the group to ever greater gaiety.

'Do you know the tune "The shepherd dressed himself up for the dance"?' Philine cried out.

'Oh yes,' he replied; 'if you want to sing and act the song, I won't fail you.'

Philine stood up and held herself in readiness. The old man started on the melody and she sang a song which we cannot share with our readers because they might perhaps find it in poor taste or even improper.

In the meantime the company, having become ever merrier, had finished up several more bottles of wine and were beginning to become very noisy. But as our friend still had fresh in his mind the unpleasant consequences their pleasure could entail, he endeavoured to break up the proceedings; he put into the old man's hand a generous reward for his efforts, the others also contributed, they let him withdraw and rest, and promised themselves renewed pleasure from his skill in the evening.

When he had gone, Wilhelm said to Philine: 'I must admit I can find neither poetic nor ethical merit in that favourite song of yours; but if you ever perform something more tasteful in the theatre with the same spontaneity, originality and elegance, you will be sure to receive widespread and keen applause.'

'Yes,' said Philine, 'It must be a really pleasant sensation, warming yourself up with ice.'

'If you think about it,' Wilhelm said, 'how very much this man puts many an actor to shame. Did you notice how right the dramatic expression of his ballads was? Certainly there was more in the way of performance in his singing than with our stiff actors on the stage; the way many plays are put on is more like a piece of narrative, whereas these stories in music seem to offer sensuous reality.'

'You are not being fair!' Laertes put in. 'I don't see myself as a great actor or singer; but I do know that when music guides the body's movements, gives them life and at the same time prescribes the tempo, and when declamation and expression are already provided for me by the composer, I am quite a different man than when in prosaic drama I am supposed to create all that for myself in the first place and to invent for myself tempo and declamation, while, what is more, every fellow-actor can disturb me in this.'

'This much I do know,' said Melina, 'that this man does put us to shame in one respect, and indeed in an important respect. The intensity of his talents is revealed in the profit which he makes from them. He persuades us to share our meal with him, although perhaps we shall soon be embarrassed to know where our next meal is coming from. He knows how to use a little song to entice out of our pockets the money that we could be using to set ourselves up to some extent. It seems so pleasant to squander the money which could be used to provide a living for oneself and other people.'

The conversation did not take the pleasantest turn as a result of this comment. Wilhelm, at whom the reproach had in fact been directed, answered with some warmth, and Melina, who did not exactly have recourse to the greatest politeness, finally brought out his complaints in somewhat dry phrases. 'It's a fortnight since we inspected the theatre and wardrobe that have been put in pawn here, and we could have both for a reasonable sum. At the time you gave me the hope that you would give me the credit for that amount, and up to now I haven't yet seen that you have considered the matter further or have come to a decision. If you had taken the opportunity then, we should be getting on with things now. You have also not yet carried out your intention of going off, and you don't seem to me to have been saving money during this time either; at least, there are persons who are always able to provide the opportunity for it to be spent more quickly.'

This not wholly unjust reproach struck home as far as our friend was concerned. He made some sort of reply in a lively, indeed impassioned manner, and as the company were rising and dispersing, he put his hand on the door, indicating in no uncertain terms that he did not wish to remain any longer with such unfriendly and ungrateful people. He hurried downstairs in an irritated state of mind, in order to sit on a stone seat which was near the doorway of his inn, and did not notice that he had drunk more than usual, partly from pleasure, partly out of annoyance.

Chapter Twelve

After a short time, which he had spent sitting and staring ahead, disturbed by all kinds of thoughts, Philine sauntered singing out of the door of the inn, and sat down beside him, indeed it could almost be said upon him, so closely did she move up to him, leaning on his shoulders, playing with his hair, stroking him and speaking to him with the friendliest of words. She implored him to stay and not to leave her on her own in that company where she would die of boredom; she could no longer go on living under the same roof with Melina and had therefore moved over to this side.

It was in vain that he tried to repulse her and to make her

understand that he could not stay any longer nor was it permissible for him to do so. She persisted with her requests, indeed she unexpectedly put her arm round his neck and kissed him with the most lively demonstration of desire.

'Are you mad, Philine?' Wilhelm exclaimed, as he attempted to disentangle himself: 'making the open street the witness of such caresses, which I in no way deserve! Let me go, I can't and won't stay.'

'And I shall hold you fast,' she said, 'and I shall go on kissing you here in the open street until you promise me what I want. I shall kill myself laughing,' she went on; 'after this familiarity the people are sure to think that I've been your wife for four weeks, and the husbands who see such an agreeable scene will praise me to their wives as a model of childishly uninhibited affection.'

Some people went by just then, and she fondled him most charmingly, and in order not to cause a scandal, he was compelled to play the role of the forbearing husband. Then she pulled faces at people's backs and high-spiritedly displayed all sorts of impudence until at last he had to promise that he would stay on today and tomorrow and the day after tomorrow.

'You are a stick!' she then said, as she let him be, 'and I'm a fool to waste so much friendliness on you.' She got up in an irritated frame of mind and walked a few paces; then she turned back laughingly and called: 'I do believe that's why I'm crazy about you; I will just go and fetch the stocking that I'm knitting, so that I've got something to do. Just stay here so that I shall find the stone man on the stone bench again.'

This time she was doing him an injustice: for, however much he tried to hold himself back from her, if he had found himself with her in a lonely bower, he probably would not have let her caresses remain unrequited at that moment.

She went into the house, after casting him a frivolous glance. He had no call to follow her, for her behaviour on the other hand had aroused in him a new reluctance; however, he got up from the seat to go after her, without really knowing why.

He was just going to enter the doorway when Melina came along, speaking to him in modest tones and begging his pardon for some phrases which had been uttered too harshly in the course of their argument. 'Don't take it amiss,' he continued, 'if in the circumstances in which I find myself, I perhaps show myself in too fearful a light; but caring for a wife, and soon perhaps for a child, stops me from one day to the next from living quietly and spending my time in the pleasure of agreeable emotions, as is still permitted to you. Think it over, and if it is possible for you to do it, put me in the possession of the theatre which is available here. I shan't be your debtor for long and will be eternally grateful to you.'

Wilhelm, who did not like to be held up on the threshold across which at this moment an irresistible attraction to Philine was drawing him, said with surprised distractedness and in hasty, good-natured mood: 'If I can make you happy and contented in this way, I shan't hesitate any longer. Go along there and settle things. I shall be ready to pay the money this very evening or early next morning.' At this he gave Melina his hand as a confirmation of his promise and was very content when he saw him hurrying away across the street; but unfortunately he was held back from entering the house a second time, and in a more unpleasant way.

A young man with a bundle on his back came hurriedly along the road and stepped up to Wilhelm who at once recognized him as Friedrich.

'Here I am again,' he cried out, as he let his big blue eyes dart joyfully around and up at all the windows; 'where is Mamsell? The devil himself can carry on any longer in the world without seeing her!'

The innkeeper, who had just approached, replied: 'She is upstairs,' and with a few leaps he was up the stairs, while Wilhelm stayed as if rooted on the threshold. For the first few moments he had felt like pulling the boy backwards by the hair down the stairs; then the intense spasm of violent jealousy suddenly put a check to the course of his life spirit and his ideas, and as he gradually recovered from his numbness, he was overcome by a disquiet and discomfort, the likes of which he had not hitherto felt in his life.

He went to his room and found Mignon busily concerned with writing. For some time recently the child had been trying with great industry to write down everything that she knew by heart, and had given to her lord and friend what she had written, so that it might be corrected. She was untiring and understood well; but the letters remained unequal and the lines crooked. Here too her body seemed to be at variance with her mind. Wilhelm, whom the child's attentions made very happy, when he was quiet in mind, paid little attention this time to what she was showing him; she sensed this and was all the more downcast about it as she believed that this time she had done her task really well.

Wilhelm's restlessness drove him up and down the corridors of the building, and back again soon to the door of the house. A rider came galloping up; he had a good appearance and for all his mature years still showed quite a lot of sprightliness. The innkeeper hastened towards him, offered him his hand as if to a known friend and called: 'Now sir, master of the horse, so we see you here once more?'

'I only want to give them fodder here,' the stranger replied, 'I've got to go at once to the estate, to have all sorts of things arranged with speed. The Count is coming tomorrow with his lady, they are going to be in residence over there for a time, in order to offer the best of hospitality to the Prince of ——, who is likely to be setting up his headquarters in this area.'

'It's a pity that you can't stay with us,' the innkeeper answered; we've got good company.' The groom, who came riding up behind, took the horse from the equerry who was conversing with the innkeeper in the doorway and was looking at Wilhelm from one side.

When the latter noticed that he was being talked about, he went away and walked up and down some of the streets.

Chapter Thirteen

In the irritating restlessness that now befell him, he had the idea of looking up the old man, hoping to be able to disperse the evil spirits by means of the latter's harp. When he inquired about the man, he was directed to a poor inn in a remote corner of the little town, and in the inn itself he was shown up the stairs to the attic from where the harp's sweet tones resounded from a small room. There were moving, plaintive notes, accompanied by sad, timid singing. Wilhelm crept up to the door, and as the good old man was giving a kind of improvisation and kept on repeating a few stanzas, partly singing them and partly reciting them, the listener, after paying attention a little while, could make out something like the following:

The man who never ate his bread
With tears, nor spent nocturnal hours
In careworn weeping on his bed,
Cannot have known you, heavenly powers.

You lead us into the midst of life,
You let poor wretches lose their worth,

And then you leave them to grief's knife,
For guilt is always avenged on earth.

The melancholy, heart-felt lament penetrated deeply into the listener's spirit. It seemed to him as if on many an occasion the old man were being prevented by tears from carrying on; then the strings would sound on their own until the voice joined in again quietly with broken tones. Wilhelm stood by the door-post, his soul was deeply stirred, the stranger's grief opened his own uneasy heart; he did not resist the feeling of sympathy, and he could not, nor did he wish to, restrain the tears which the old man's moving lament finally drew from his eyes too. All the sorrows that were pressing upon his heart were dissolved at the same time, he abandoned himself completely to them, pushed open the attic door and stood before the old man, who had been compelled to be seated upon a wretched bed, the only furniture in this poor dwelling-place.

'What emotions you have stirred up in me, good old man!' he exclaimed. 'You have dissolved all those things which were congealed in my heart; don't let me disturb you, but continue to make a friend happy while you alleviate your own sufferings.' The old man wanted to get up and say something, but Wilhelm prevented him from doing this; for he had noticed at midday that the man was reluctant to speak; he preferred to sit down beside him on the straw-mattress.

The old man dried his eyes and asked with a friendly smile: 'How did you get here? I was thinking of calling to attend on you again this evening.'

'It's quieter for us here,' Wilhelm replied; 'sing to me anything you like, whatever fits into your situation, and behave simply as if I were not here. It seems to me as if you couldn't go wrong today. I think you are very lucky to be able to occupy and entertain yourself so pleasantly in solitude and, as you are everywhere a stranger, to find the most agreeable form of acquaintance within your own heart.'

The old man glanced at the strings of his instrument, and after he had played a few notes as a prelude, tuned up and sang:

The man who yields to solitude
Alas, is soon alone;
With living and loving all are imbued,
And they leave him free to moan.
Yes, leave me to my pain.
If I can once more remain
Upon my own,
I'm not then all alone.

A lover quietly goes on his way,
Will his mistress be on her own?
Thus grief comes upon me night and day,
And I'm left alone to moan,
And I'm left alone to my pain.
But once I can remain
In my grave upon my own,
My grief will leave me alone.

We would become too discursive, and yet not be able to give expression to the charm of the strange conversation which our friend had with the odd stranger. All that the young man said to him the old man answered with the purest agreement by means of harmonies which stirred all cognate emotions and opened up a broad field to the imagination.

Anyone who has been present at a meeting of pious people who believe that they worship more purely, more sincerely and more intelligently when they are separated from the church, will be able to form an idea of the present scene; he will remember how the liturgist is able to adjust to his own words the verse of a song which lifts up the heart in the direction in which the speaker wishes it to take its flight, how soon after another person from the congregation adds in another melody the verse of another song, and how to this a third again links up a third, with the result that the related ideas of the songs from which they are borrowed are certainly aroused, though each passage becomes new and individual by means of the new association, as if it had been invented at that very moment; and as a result of this there arises out of a familiar circle of ideas, out of familiar songs and sayings, for this particular society, for this moment, a specific whole through the enjoyment of which this society is enlivened, fortified and refreshed. Thus the old man acted improvingly upon his guest when he brought into circulation pleasant and painful emotions, from which in the present circumstances of our friend the best was to be expected, through songs and passages known and unknown, through close and distant feelings, and emotions that were waking and sleeping, pleasant and painful.

Chapter Fourteen

On the way back indeed he really began to think about his position in a more vigorous manner than he had done hitherto, and had reached home with the intention of extricating himself out of this situation when the innkeeper immediately told him in confidence that Miss Philine had made a conquest of the Count's master of horse, for the latter had returned with the greatest speed, after fulfilling his task on the estate, and was enjoying a good dinner with her upstairs in her room.

At this moment Melina entered with the notary; they went up together to Wilhelm's room, where the latter made good his promise, although with some hesitation, paid out three hundred talers in a bill of exchange to Melina who at once handed it over to the notary and received in return a document about the completion of purchase of all the theatrical equipment which was to be handed over to him the next day.

They had scarcely separated when Wilhelm heard a terrible cry in the house. He heard a youthful voice, angry and threatening, which made itself heard through unrestrained weeping and crying. He could hear this lament coursing from high up to down below, past his own room and down into the yard of the inn.

When curiosity had enticed our friend downstairs, he found Friedrich in a kind of frenzy. The boy wept, ground his teeth, stamped his feet, threatened with clenched fists and was behaving in a quite unruly way in his anger and annoyance, Mignon stood facing him and was looking on with astonishment, and it was the innkeeper who gave some kind of explanation for this happening.

Apparently the boy had been contented, merry and cheerful on his return, when Philine had received him welcomingly, and had been singing and leaping around up to the time when the master of horse had made Philine's acquaintance. Now this fellow, who was something between a child and a youth, had begun to show his annoyance, banging the doors and rushing up and down. Philine had ordered him to wait at table that evening, at which he had only become more sullen and defiant; finally, instead of putting a dish of stew on the table, he had thrown it between Philine and the guest, who had been sitting quite close together, after which the master of horse had boxed his ears soundly a few times and thrown him out of the room. Then the innkeeper reported that he had helped both persons to clean themselves, since their clothes had been badly soiled.

When the boy heard about the good effect of his revenge, he began to laugh out loud, though the tears were still running down his cheeks. For some time he was really pleased until he recalled the indignity inflicted upon him by the stronger man, and then he started once more to howl and be abusive.

Wilhelm was thoughtful and abashed as he witnessed this scene. He saw here a delineation of his most inward self, presented with sharp and exaggerated lines; he too had been enflamed by an insuperable fit of jealousy; he too, had not propriety restrained him, would have been glad to give rein to his wild mood, to have hurt the object of his love with malicious pleasure and to have challenged his rival; he would have gladly destroyed those people who only seemed to be there in order to annoy him.

Laertes, who had also come along and heard the story, roguishly supported the infuriated boy when the latter asserted and avowed that the master of horse must give him satisfaction, for he had never up to now taken any insult lying down; if the master of horse should refuse, he would know how to avenge himself.

Laertes was right in his own line here. He went upstairs in earnest mood, in order to challenge the master of horse in the boy's name.

'That's amusing,' the latter said; 'I hadn't imagined I should have this sort of fun this evening.' They went down, and Philine followed them. 'My son', the master of horse said to Friedrich, 'you are a good lad, and I'm not refusing to fight with you; only as the inequality of our ages and strength makes the business rather fantastic in any case, I suggest rapiers, not other weapons; we will mark the buttons with chalk, and the one who plants the first hit, or the most hits, on the other's coat is to be deemed the winner and to be treated by the other one to the best wine that can be had in the town.'

Laertes decided that this suggestion could be accepted; Friedrich obeyed him as his instructor. The rapiers were brought along, Philine sat down with some knitting and looked at the two contenders with great equanimity.

The master of horse, who fought very well, was obliging enough to be sparing towards his opponent and to allow a few chalk-marks to be made on his coat, after which they embraced, and wine was brought in. The master of horse wanted to know about Friedrich's origins and his story, and the latter then told a fairy-story that he had often repeated already and which we think of relating to our readers some other time.

In Wilhelm's soul meanwhile this duel completed the delineation of his own feelings; for he could not deny to himself that he himself would have liked to direct a rapier, indeed preferably a dagger, against the master of horse, even though he realized that the latter was far superior to him in the art of fencing. However, he did not deign to glance at Philine, restrained himself from any comment that might have betrayed his emotions, and after drinking a number of times to the health of the contestants, he hastened up to his room where a thousand disagreeable thoughts pressed upon him.

He remembered the time when his spirit had been uplifted by unquestioning, hopeful striving, and when he used to swim in the liveliest enjoyment of all kind as if in an element. He became aware how he had now got into a vague, lounging mood in which he only tasted in sips what formerly he had absorbed in full draughts; but he could not see clearly what insuperable need had been made into a law for him by nature, and how much this need had only been stimulated, half satisfied and misled by circumstances.

Therefore no one need be surprised if Wilhelm became very confused when he looked at his position and endeavoured to think his way out of it. It was not enough that he should be detained through his friendship for Laertes, his liking for Philine and his sympathy for Mignon longer than was reasonable in a place and with a group of people where he could cherish his favourite taste, could satisfy his wishes, as it were surreptitiously, and without setting himself any purpose to work for, could slink after his old dreams. He believed he had sufficient strength to cut loose from these relationships and to make a break at once. But now only a few moments earlier he had become involved in a business deal with Melina and had made the acquaintance of the enigmatic old man whose mystery he wished with ineffable longing to decipher. Only after thoughts that had moved in various directions, had he made up his mind, or at least believed he had made up his mind, that he would not let himself be held back by these things either. 'I must get away,' he exclaimed, 'I will get away!' He flung himself on to a chair and was very disturbed. Mignon came in and asked him if she could help with his hair. She came softly; it wounded her deeply that he had treated her so abruptly earlier in the day.

Nothing is more moving that when a love which has nourished itself quietly and a loyalty that has been confirmed privately at last come close at the right hour to the person who up to now has not been worthy of them, and are revealed to him. The bud that had for a long time been austerely closed was ready, and Wilhelm's heart could not be more receptive.

She stood before him and saw his disquiet.—'Sir,' she called out, 'if you are unhappy, what is to become of Mignon?'—'Dear creature,' he said, taking her hands, 'you too are part of my sadness. I have to go away.'—She looked into his eyes, which were glittering with suppressed tears, and knelt down impulsively before him. He still held her hands, she had laid her head on his knees and was completely still. He played with her hair and was friendly. For a long time she stayed quiet. At last he felt a kind of twitching in her, which began quite gently, and extended and grew through all her limbs.—'What's the matter, Mignon?' he cried out, 'What's the matter?'—She lifted up her little head and looked at him, suddenly feeling for her heart, as if with a gesture which is stifling pain. He lifted her up, and she fell upon his lap; he pressed her to himself and kissed her. She did not reply by any pressure of the hand or by any movement. She held tightly on to her heart, and all at once she uttered a cry which was accompanied by spasms. She started up and then at once collapsed in front of him, as if broken in all her limbs. It was a horrifying sight.—'My child!', he called out, lifting her up and embracing her, 'My child, what is it?'—The convulsions continued, emanating from the heart to the trembling limbs; she simply hung in his arms. He clasped her to his arms and moistened her with his tears. Suddenly she seemed under tension again, like someone who is undergoing the most acute physical pain; and soon all her limbs came alive again with a new fierceness, and she threw her arms around his neck, like a spring that snaps to, while in her innermost being something like a mighty rent took place, and at that moment a stream of tears flowed from her closed eyes into his bosom. He held her fast. She wept, and no tongue can speak of the violence of these tears. Her long hair had come untied and was hanging down from her as she wept, and her whole being seemed to be melting away irresistibly into a stream of tears. Her rigid limbs became limp, her most inward self was pouring forth, and in the confusion of the moment Wilhelm was afraid that she would melt away in his arms and that he would be left with nothing of her. He held her all the more tightly.—'My child!' he cried, 'my child! You are indeed mine, if this word can be of any comfort to you. You are mine! I shall keep you, I won't leave you!'—Her tears continued to flow.—'My father!' she cried, 'you won't leave me! You will be my father! I am your child!'

Outside the door the harp could be heard sounding quietly; the old man was bringing his most deeply felt songs as an evening offering to the friend who, holding his child ever more firmly in his arms, enjoyed the purest, most indescribable happiness.

BOOK THREE

Chapter One

Know you the land where lemons are in flower,
Where the golden oranges glow in the dusky bower,
A gentle wind descends from the azure sky,
The myrtle is still and the laurel stretches high,
Is it known to you?
Oh there, yes, there,
Beloved, goes the way that you and I should share.

Know you the house, whose roof and pillars rose,
The hall is bright with light, the small room glows,
And marble figures hold me in their view:
Oh you poor child, what have they done to you?
Is it known to you?
Oh there, yes there,
Protector, goes the way that you and I should share.

Know you the heights and the pathway through the clouds?
The mule seeks out its track in misty shrouds,
The dragons' ancient brood lives in the caves,
The rocks fall sheer, and over them the waves:
Is it known to you?
Oh there, yes there,
O father, goes the way that you and I must share.

When next morning Wilhelm looked around in the house for Mignon, he could not find her, but heard that she had gone out early with Melina, who had set out in good time in order to take possession of the wardrobe and the rest of the theatre equipment.

After a few hours had passed, Wilhelm heard music outside his door. At first he thought that the Harpist was already there again; but soon he could make out the sound of a zither, and the voice which began to sing was Mignon's. Wilhelm opened the door, the child stepped in and sang the song which we have just noted down.

Our friend liked in particular the melody and the expression, although he could not understand all the words. He asked for the verses to be repeated and explained, wrote them down and translated them into German. But he could only give a remote imitation of the originality of the phrases; the childlike innocence of expression disappeared as the broken speech was made consistent, and what was disjointed was linked together. Furthermore, the charm of the melody was incomparable.

She began each verse in a grand and solemn manner, as if she wanted to draw attention to something special, and as if she wished to recite something important. At the third line the song became more muffled and sombre; she gave a mysterious and cautious expression to the question 'Is it known to you?'; there was an irresistible yearning in the phrase 'Oh there, yes there', and she knew how to vary the words 'the way that you and I should share' at each repetition in such a way that at one time they were pleading and urgent, at another persuasive and promising.

After she had finished the song for the second time she paused a moment, looked sharply at Wilhelm and asked: 'Do you know the land?' 'It must be Italy that is meant,' answered Wilhelm; 'Where did you learn the little song?' 'Italy!' Mignon said in a significant manner; 'if you go to Italy, take me with you, I'm freezing here.' 'Have you already been there, my little darling?' Wilhelm asked. The child stayed quiet, and nothing further could be got out of her.

Melina, who came in just then, looked at the zither and was pleased that it had already been put into such good repair. The instrument was part of the inventory of the old theatre wardrobe. Mignon had asked for it that morning, the Harpist restrung it immediately, and the child developed with this opportunity a gift which up to then she had not been known to have.

Melina had already taken over the theatre wardrobe and all that went with it; some members of the town council at once promised that he would have permission to perform in the locality for some time to come. So he came back again with a light heart and a cheerful countenance; for he was gentle and polite to everyone, indeed obliging and engaging. He congratulated himself that he would now be able to give work to his friends, who up to now had been embarrassed and idle, and to take them on for a time, though at the same time he regretted that at first certainly he would not be able to reward according to their capacities and talents the first-rate people that good fortune had led his way, since before everything else he must pay off what he owed to such a generous friend as Wilhelm had shown himself to be.

'I can't tell you what great friendship you are showing me by helping me to become manager of a theatre. For when I first met you I was in a very strange situation. You will remember how when we first became acquainted I revealed to you my dislike of the theatre, and yet I had to look around for an engagement as soon as I was married, because of my love for my wife who was looking forward to much pleasure and acclaim from the stage. I didn't find any engagement, at least nothing permanent, but fortunately I did meet some business people who in exceptional circumstances were able to make use of someone who knew how to use a pen, who had some French and was not wholly inexperienced in accounts. In this way things went quite well for me for a time, I was tolerably paid, bought myself a number of things, and my circumstances were no discredit to me. But the exceptional contracts from my patrons came to an end, there was no question of a permanent living, and my wife longed all the more keenly for the theatre, unfortunately at a time when her circumstances are not the most advantageous for showing herself to the public in a creditable light. I hope now that the establishment which I am going to set up with your help will be a good start for me and mine, and it is to you that I owe my future happiness, however it may turn out.'

Wilhelm heard these remarks with satisfaction, and all the actors were likewise pretty satisfied with the new manager's declarations, were secretly pleased that an engagement was so quickly forthcoming, and were disposed to accept a small salary in the first place, because most of them regarded what had been offered to them so unexpectedly as a contribution which they had not been able to count on a short while earlier. Melina was about to take advantage of this situation, made efforts in a clever manner to have a word with everyone separately, and was able to persuade the one in this way and the other in that, so that they were disposed to sign the contracts quickly without thinking much about the new relationship, and believing themselves to be sufficiently insured if they could get away again by giving six weeks' notice.

Now the conditions were to be drawn up in the appropriate way, and Melina was already thinking about the plays with which he wanted firstly to entice the public, when a messenger came to tell the master of horse of the impending arrival of their lordships, and the master of horse ordered the horses which had been got ready to be brought forward.

Soon afterwards the carriage drove up to the inn; it was packed high with luggage, and two servants jumped down from the driver's seat; as was her way, Philine was immediately at hand, placing herself in the doorway.

'Who might you be?' the Countess asked as she stepped in.

'An actress, if it pleases your excellency,' was the reply as she roguishly bowed and kissed the lady's cloak with a really devout expression and humble gestures.

Seeing further persons standing around who likewise proclaimed themselves as actors, the Count inquired about the size of the troupe, the last place where they had been, and their manager. 'If they had been French,' he said to his wife, 'we would have given the Prince an unexpected pleasure and have provided him with his favourite entertainment.'

'The question is whether we shouldn't have these people, even if unfortunately they are only Germans, to perform at the house for as long as the Prince is staying with us,' the Countess rejoined. 'After all, they surely will have a certain skill. A large gathering of people can be best entertained by a theatre-company, and the Baron would lick them into shape all right.'

While this was being said, they went up the steps, and Melina presented himself at the top as manager. 'Call your people together,' the Count said, 'and introduce them to me, so that I can see what they're like. At the same time I also want to see the list of the plays which they could put on, if need be.'

With a deep bow Melina hurried out of the room and returned soon with the actors. They pressed in front of and behind one another; some showed themselves in a poor light because of a great desire to please, and the others did not do any better because they presented themselves in a frivolous manner. Philine showed complete respect to the Countess who was extraordinarily gracious and friendly; meanwhile the Count mustered the others. He asked each of them about the role he played, and commented to Melina that it was necessary to stick closely to one's roles, a saying which the latter received with great devotion.

The Count then commented to everyone about what they particularly needed to study, how their figure and stance could be improved, showed them clearly where the Germans always went wrong, and displayed such unusual knowledge that everybody stood in the greatest humility before such a distinguished connoisseur and protector and scarcely dared to draw breath.

'Who is that fellow in the corner over there?' the Count asked, as he looked at a person who had not yet been introduced to him, and a thin figure approached, dressed in a threadbare coat with patched elbows; a poor sort of wig covered the head of the humble fellow.

This person, whom we know already from the previous book as Philine's favourite, usually played the part of pedant, schoolmaster or poet, and took over for the most part the role when somebody had to be beaten or to have something poured over him. He had got into the way of bowing in a certain subservient, ridiculous and fearful manner, and his hesitant speech which was suited to his roles made audiences laugh, so that he was still regarded as a useful member of the company, particularly as he was moreover very obliging and complaisant. He approached the Count in his own style, bowed to him, and answered every question in the manner in which he was accustomed to presenting his roles on the stage. The Count looked at him for a time with agreeable attention and consideration, then he called out, turning to the Countess: 'My child, do look carefully at this man; I'll guarantee he is a great actor, or going to become one.' The fellow made a silly bow in all seriousness, so that the Count could not help bursting out laughing loudly at him, crying out: 'He performs his tasks excellently! I bet this man can take on any part he likes, and it's a shame that he hasn't been used for anything better up to now.'

Such extraordinary favour was very hurtful to the others; it was only Melina who did not sense any of this, on the contrary he declared the Count to be completely right and added respectfully: 'Oh yes, all we've been missing is such an expert and such encouragement as we have found at present in Your Excellency.'

'Is that the entire company?' the Count said.

'A few members are absent', clever Melina interspersed, 'and in any case, we could very soon be at full strength, if only we could find patronage.'

Meanwhile Philine said to the Countess: 'There is another really handsome, young man upstairs, who would certainly soon qualify to play the first lover.'

'Why doesn't he show himself?' the Countess rejoined.

'I'll fetch him,' cried Philine, and she hurried out at the door.

She found Wilhelm still occupied with Mignon and persuaded him to go down with her. He followed her with some misgivings, but curiosity impelled him on; for when he heard speak of aristocratic personages, he was full of eagerness to get to know them more closely. He stepped into the room, and his eyes at once met the Countess' eyes, which were turned towards him. Philine took him to the lady, while the Count was concerned with the others. Wilhelm bowed, and not without some confusion replied to various questions which the charming lady put to him. Her beauty, youth, grace, delicacy and good manners made the pleasantest of impressions upon him, the more so, as her speech and gestures were accompanied by a certain modesty, indeed one might say embarrassment. He was also introduced to the Count, but the latter paid little attention to him, rather stepping to the window with his wife where he appeared to be asking her for something. It could be seen that her opinion concurred with his in the liveliest way, indeed, that she seemed to be asking something of him imploringly and to be confirming him in his own viewpoint.

Soon afterwards he returned to the company and said: 'I can't stay any longer at present, but I will send a friend to you, and if your conditions are reasonable and you are prepared to put in quite a lot of effort, I am not averse to letting you perform at the castle.'

All showed their great pleasure at this, and Philine in particular kissed the Countess' hands with the greatest vivacity.

'Look, little one,' the lady said, as she tapped the frivolous girl on the cheeks, 'look, my child, there you are, coming to me again; I will keep my promise all right, only you must dress better.' Philine excused herself, saying that she had little to spend on her wardrobe, and immediately the Countess ordered her maids to hand to her an English hat and silk scarf which were easy to unpack. Now the Countess herself decked out Philine who continued to comport and behave herself very properly with a misleading and innocent facial expression.

The Count offered the Countess his hand and escorted her downstairs. As she went past, she greeted the whole company in a friendly manner and again turned round to Wilhelm, saying to him with the most gracious mien: 'We'll see each other again soon.'

Such fortunate prospects enlivened the whole company: everyone now gave free rein to his hopes, wishes and imaginings, talked about the parts he would like to play and about the applause he would like to receive. Melina considered how he could still quickly get some money from the inhabitants of the little town by giving some performances and at the same time keep the company busy, while others went into the kitchen with a view to ordering a better lunch than they had been used to having.

Chapter Two

After a few days the Baron came, and it was not without trepidation the Melina received him. The Count had announced him as a connoisseur, and it was a cause of worry that he would find the weaknesses of the little group and be aware that he was not dealing with an established company, since they could scarcely find the proper cast for a single play; but manager and entire company as well were soon relieved of all anxiety, as they found in the Baron a man who regarded the German-based theatre with the greatest enthusiasm and to whom every actor and every troupe were welcome and a source of pleasure. He greeted them all solemnly, considered himself fortunate to have come across a German company so unexpectedly, to be associated with it, and to be introducing the indigenous Muses into his relative's castle. Soon after this he took out of his pocket a copy-book in which Melina hoped to see the particulars of the contract; but it was something quite different. The Baron asked them to listen attentively to a play that he had written himself and which he would like to see them act. They gladly formed a circle and were pleased to be able to ensure the favour of so necessary a man at so little cost, although they all feared it would take an excessively long time, judging from the thickness of the book. It really was so too; the play was written in five acts and of the sort that never comes to an end.

The hero was a refined, virtuous and generous-minded man, who was at the same time misunderstood and persecuted, but who none the less did finally triumph over his enemies who would then have been exposed to the most severe form of poetic justice, if he had not forgiven them on the spot.

While this play was being read aloud, each listener had opportunity enough to think of himself and to move up quite gently from the humility to which he felt inclined only a short time earlier to a pleasurable complacency and from there to survey the prospects for the future as being most agreeable. Those who could not find a suitable role for themselves in the play judged it in their own minds as a bad one and considered the Baron to be an ill-fated author, whereas the others paid attention with the greatest praises to an episode, in which they hoped to be applauded, so that the author should feel as pleased as possible.

They soon settled the business side of the arrangements. Melina was able to conclude the contract with the Baron to his own advantage and to keep it secret from the other actors.

Melina mentioned Wilhelm to the Baron in passing and assured him that he would make a very good playwright and was not at all badly qualified even to be an actor. The Baron at once made acquaintance with him as with a colleague, and Wilhelm brought out a few little plays which had been saved by chance, along with a few other relics, on that day when he had consigned the greater part of his writings to the flames. The Baron praised the plays as well as the delivery, assumed that it was known that he would be coming over to the castle with them, and promised as he took leave that they would all have the best of receptions, comfortable accommodation, good food, applause and presents, while Melina added to these the assurance of a certain amount of pocket-money.

It can be imagined how this visit had put the company in a good mood, in that they saw all at once the prospect of respect and comfort instead of worrying and lowly circumstances. They were already making merry in anticipation of that account, and everyone thought it inappropriate to keep any pennies further in their pockets.

In the meantime Wilhelm was considering whether he should accompany the troupe to the castle, and found it advisable to go there for more reasons than one. Melina was hoping that this advantageous contract would enable him to pay off at least part of his debt, and our friend, who was in search of knowledge of human nature, did not want to miss the opportunity of getting to know more closely the great world, in which he hoped to acquire much information about life, about himself and about art. At the same time he dared not admit to himself how much he wished to come more closely again to the beautiful Countess. He rather tried to convince himself in general terms about what great advantages he would obtain from a better knowledge of the world of elegance and wealth. He made his own observations about the Count, the Countess and the Baron, about the assurance, ease and graciousness of their manners, and when he was on his own he cried out with rapture:

'Those whose birth raises them at once above the lower grades of humanity are to be acclaimed as three times fortunate; they do not need to go through those conditions in which many good people have to fret their whole life through, nor do they even need to linger there as visitors. Their gaze, directed to the higher point of view, must be in general terms and rightly focused, and each step in their life must be an easy one! From birth onwards they are, as it were, given a place on a ship in order that they can make use of the favourable winds and await the passing of the adverse ones in the voyage which we must all make, whereas other people wear themselves out swimming simply on their own, are unable to gain much advantage from favourable winds and go under in the storm, their strength being soon exhausted. What convenience and ease are provided by inherited wealth! And how securely does one enterprise flourish which is based on good capital investment, so that not every unsuccessful venture results straightaway in inactivity! Who can know better the value and vanity of earthly things than someone who has been in a position to enjoy them from childhood onwards, and who can direct his mind at an earlier stage on to what is necessary, useful and true than someone who has to convince himself about so many errors at an age when he still has the strength to start a new life!'

It was in these terms that our friend wished luck to all those who should find themselves in the higher regions; but he also wished well to those who might be approaching such a sphere and might be able to draw sustenance from these sources, and he gave praise to his own protective spirit that was preparing to lead him too up these steps.

In the meantime, after he had puzzled himself for a long time as to how he might divide the company, according to the Count's wishes and his own convictions, into special groups and how he might assign to each his particular form of co-operation, Melina had to count himself very lucky, when it came to putting things into practice, if with such a small personnel he found the actors willing to adapt themselves as far as possible for various roles. Usually, however, Laertes took on the lovers, Philine the chambermaids, the two young women separated themselves as the naive and the tender women in love, and the blustering old fellow was played best. Melina believed that he could appear most suitably as a nobleman, whereas Madame Melina, to her great annoyance, had to transfer to the category of young women, indeed even of fond mothers, and since a pedant or poet, if there should be one at all, is not made to look ridiculous in the more modern plays, the known favourite of the Count now had to play the presidents and ministers, because these are usually introduced as villains and have a rough time in the fifth act. Similarly Melina took pleasure as gentleman of the bedchamber or chamberlain in pocketing the insults which were pressed upon him in various popular plays by good honest German men, because he could none the less use the opportunity to dress himself up prettily and was entitled to assume the manner of a courtier, which he believed he possessed completely.

It was not long before several actors came along from various directions; they were taken on without special auditions, but also without special conditions.

Wilhelm, whom Melina had tried to persuade several times, but in vain, to accept an acting part as a young man in love, applied himself to the business with much good will, without our new manager acknowledging his efforts in the least; on the contrary,

Melina believed that in obtaining his new office he had also required all necessary insight; making cuts was in particular one of his favourite occupations, and in this way he knew how to reduce any play to the right length, as far as time was concerned, but without taking any other factors into consideration. He was much sought after, the audiences were very satisfied, and those inhabitants of the little town who had the most taste maintained that the theatre in the capital was by no means in such good shape as theirs.

Chapter Three

At last the time came when preparations for the move were to be made, when the coaches and carriages were expected which had been ordered to conduct our whole company to the Count's residence. Already beforehand great arguments took place as to who was to travel with whom and how people would sit. The ordering and dividing out were in the end settled and established only with difficulty, but unfortunately without effect. At the agreed time fewer carriages arrived than had been expected, and it was necessary to manage accordingly. The Baron, following not long afterwards on horseback, gave as reason that everything in the house was in a great turmoil because not only would the Prince arrive a few days earlier than anticipated, but also because unexpected guests had already arrived; there was a shortage of space, and they would not therefore have such good accommodation as had been previously arranged for them, for which he was extremely sorry.

They divided themselves into the carriages as well as they could, and as the weather was tolerable and the castle was only a few hours away, the cheeriest amongst them preferred to set out on foot rather than to wait for the carriages to come back. The convoy set out with joyful shouts, and for the first time they were without worry about paying bills. The Count's place stood like a fairy castle before their mind's eye, they were the most joyful and cheerful people on earth, and every one of them, while on the journey, linked to this day a succession of fortunate, honorific and prosperous happenings, dependent on their individual ways of thinking.

A heavy downpour of rain, which came about unexpectedly,

could not deflect them from their pleasant feelings; but as it became more and more persistent and marked, many of them did become aware of a certain discomfort. Night fell, and nothing could seem more desirable to them than the Count's palace, lit up on all storeys as it gleamed towards them from a hill so that they could count the windows.

When they came closer, they also found all the windows of the annexes illuminated. Each of them wondered to himself which would in fact be his room, and mostly they contented themselves modestly with a little room in the attic or the wings.

They now went through the village past the inn. Wilhelm asked the convoy to stop so that he could get out; but the innkeeper made it clear that there was not any space at all that he could provide for him. As unexpected guests had arrived, the Count had at once booked the whole inn, and yesterday already all the rooms had been clearly marked with chalk to indicate who was to occupy them. Consequently our friend, against his will, had to drive into the courtyard of the house with the rest of the company.

They could see busy cooks moving this way and that around the kitchen fires in a side-building, and their spirits were raised just by the sight of this; servants carrying lights were hastening up the steps of the main building, and the good travellers' spirits rose at the prospect. How very surprised they were on the other hand when this reception turned into terrible cursing. The servants swore at the drivers for having come in this way; they should turn round and go out again to the old house, someone called out, there was no room for these guests here! They added all sorts of jeering remarks to this so unfriendly and unexpected news, and laughed their fill that they had been brought into the rain because of this mistake. It was still pouring, there were no stars in the sky, and now the company were led by a rough road between two walls into the old house at the back which had been standing empty since the Count's father had built the one in front. The coaches halted partly in the courtyard and partly beneath a long, arched gateway, and the drivers, farmers from the village, unharnessed the horses and went their ways.

As nobody appeared to receive the troupe, they descended, called out, and searched round; but in vain. Everything remained dark and quiet. The wind was blowing through the empty gateway, and the old towers and courtyards, whose shapes they could scarcely make out in the dark, caused shudders of fear. They froze and shivered, the women were afraid, the children began to cry, their impatience mounted each moment, and such a quick change of fortune, for which no one had been prepared, was completely upsetting for them all.

As they expected every minute that someone would come and open up for them, and as now rain, now storm deceived them and they believed more than once that they could hear the steps of the longed-for house steward, they remained disconsolate and inactive for a long time; it did not occur to anyone to go into the new house and there to implore sympathetic souls for help. They could not understand what had happened to their friend the Baron, and were in a highly awkward situation.

At last some people really came, and from their voices they recognized them as those walkers who had remained behind the ones who had come by coach. They reported that the Baron had had a fall with his horse and had severely injured his foot, and that when they had asked in the house they too had been directed here with summary impetuosity.

The whole company was in the greatest embarrassment, people debated what should be done and could come to no conclusion. At last they saw a lantern approaching from the distance, and drew breath again; but the hope of a speedy solution disappeared again when the phenomenon came closer and became clear. A groom with a light preceded the Count's master of horse, who is known to us, and the latter, when he came nearer, inquired very eagerly about Miss Philine. She had scarcely stepped forward from the rest of the crowd when he very pressingly offered to conduct her to the new building, where a little place had been found for her with the lady's maids of the Countess. She did not hesitate long before accepting the offer with thanks, she took him by the arm and wanted to hurry off with him, having recommended her trunk to the care of the others; but people got in the way, begging and imploring the master of the horse, with the result that in the end he promised all and everything, if only in order to be able to make off with his beautiful lady, and gave the assurance that the house would be opened very soon and that they would be accommodated in the best possible manner. Soon afterwards they saw the glow of his lantern disappear and for a long time hoped in vain for the new light which did finally appear after much waiting, scolding and cursing, and kindled in them some consolation and hope.

An old manservant opened the door of the old building, into which they pressed forward with vehemence. Everyone now paid attention to his own things, getting down the cases and bringing them in. Most of the pieces were thoroughly soaked, like the people themselves. With only one light everything took a long time. Inside the building they knocked against things, stumbled and fell. More lights were asked for, and fuel for heating. The monosyllabic servant could only just be persuaded to leave his lamp behind; he went, and did not come back again.

Now they began to search through the house; all the room doors were open; great stoves, woven tapestries and inlaid floors still remained to testify to the building's former splendour, but there was no other household equipment to be found, no tables, chairs or mirrors, only a few huge empty bedsteads that had been robbed of all ornamentation and of all essentials. The wet trunks and cases were chosen as seats, some of the tired travellers made do with the floor, Wilhelm had sat down on some stairs, Mignon was lying across his knees; the child was restless, and when he asked her what was wrong, she answered: 'I'm hungry!' He could find nothing of his own to allay the child's craving, the rest of the company had also finished up all supplies, and he was compelled to leave the poor creature without refreshment. In the course of the whole episode he remained inactive, brooding quietly; for he was very annoyed and angry that he had not insisted on following his own inclination and had not alighted at the inn, even if it had meant his having to be quartered in the topmost attic.

The others behaved each in his own way. Some had collected a pile of old wood and put it in a hugh fireplace in the assembly room, setting fire to the pyre with shouts of joy. Unfortunately this hope of becoming dry and warm was also deceived most terribly, for this fireplace was only there as an ornament and had been walled in from above; the smoke quickly came back and filled the rooms all at once; the dry wood burst crackling into flames, and the flames were also driven outwards; the draught, penetrating through the broken panes of glass in the windows, gave the flames an unsteadiness of direction, they were afraid of setting fire to the house, the fire had to be dismantled, trodden down and doused, the smoke increased, conditions became unbearable, and people were coming close to despair.

Wilhelm had withdrawn from the smoke to a distant room, where Mignon soon followed him, leading in a well-dressed manservant who was carrying a high, bright and doubly lit lantern; the latter turned to Wilhelm and, as he offered him sweets and fruit on a beautiful porcelain plate, he said: 'This is sent to you by the young lady from over there, with the request that you join the company; she asked me to tell you,' the servant added with a frivolous look, 'that things are going well as far as she is concerned, and that she wishes to share her satisfaction with her friends.'

This offer was the last thing that Wilhelm was expecting, for since the adventure of the stone seat he had treated Philine with marked contempt, and had so firmly made up his mind to have no further association with her that he was on the point of sending the gift of sweetmeats back again, when a pleading look of Mignon's persuaded him to accept it and to express his thanks for it in the child's name; he totally refused the invitation. He asked the servant to have some concern for the comapny that had just arrived, and inquired after the Baron. The latter was in bed, but, as far as the servant could tell, had entrusted someone else with the task of looking after those who were being accommodated in such a wretched manner.

The servant went, leaving with Wilhelm one of his lights; as there was no candlestick, the latter had to fix it on to the window-sill, and now at least in the course of his observations he could see the four walls of the room lit up. For there was still a long time to go before arrangements were actively undertaken so that our guests should be pacified. Gradually lights came along, though without snuffers, then some chairs, an hour later bed-coverings, then pillows, all pretty well wet through,and it was already well after midnight when finally straw sacks and mattresses were brought along which, if they had been available in the first place, would have been very welcome.

In the meantime a certain amount of food and drink had also arrived which was enjoyed without much criticism, although it looked like an untidy lot of left-overs and did not offer any special testimony to the respect in which the guests were held.

Chapter Four

Because of the bad behaviour and presumption of some thoughtless fellows who teased each other, woke each other up and played all kinds of tricks on each other in turn, the disturbance and inconvenience of the night were increased. The next morning arrived, bringing loud complaints about their friend the Baron, that he had so deceived them and had given them quite a different picture of the orderliness and comfort which they would encounter. Yet to their surprise and consolation the Count himself appeared with some servants first thing and inquired how they were getting on. He was very angry when he heard how badly things had gone with them, and the Baron, who was being escorted as he limped up to them, indicted the house steward for having acted disobediently in the matter and believed that he had got him into real hot water.

The Count at once ordered that everything should be done immediately to ensure all possible comfort for the guests. After that some officers came along who immediately took cognizance of the actresses, and the Count had the whole company introduced to him, addressed each one by his name and inserted some humorous remarks into the discussion, so that everyone was really delighted at such a gracious gentleman. Finally it came to Wilhelm's turn, with Mignon clinging to him. Wilhelm excused himself, as well as he could, for the liberty he had taken, but the Count seemed to take his presence for granted.

A gentleman who was standing near the Count and who looked like an officer, although he had no uniform on, talked in particular with our friend and stood out among all the others. Large light-blue eyes gleamed beneath a high forehead, his blond hair was negligently brushed up, and with his average height he showed a very bold, firm and definite nature. His questions were lively, and he seemed to have a good understanding of everything that he asked about.

Wilhelm inquired about this man from the Baron, who, however, had not much that was good to say about him. He said that he had the title of major, was actually the Prince's favourite, carried out his most secret missions and was considered to be his right-hand man, indeed, there was reason to believe that he was his natural son. He had been with embassies in France, England and Italy, was very distinguished everywhere, and that made him conceited; he liked to think that he had a thorough knowledge of German literature and he allowed himself all kinds of shallow gibes at its expense. He, the Baron, avoided all conversation with him, and Wilhelm would do well to keep aloof from him as well, for in the final resort he made cutting remarks to everyone. He was called Jarno, but nobody rightly knew what to make of the name.

Wilhelm had nothing to say to this, for he felt somewhat drawn to the stranger, although there was something cold and repellent about him.

The company was allocated quarters in the house, and Melina gave very strict orders that they should henceforth behave properly, the women should live apart, and everyone was to concentrate his attention and inclination to his parts and to art. He put up on all doors rules and regulations which consisted of many points. The amount of the fine was fixed which every offender was to pay into a common pool.

These precepts were given little attention. Young officers went in and out, joked with the actresses, not in the most refined way, made fun of the actors and destroyed the entire little set of house rules before they could take root. There was chasing through the rooms, dressing up and hiding. Melina, who at first wanted to show some seriousness, felt driven to extremes by all kinds of mischievousness, and when soon afterwards the Count summoned him to look at the place where the theatre was to be set up, the nuisance only became all the worse. The young gentlemen thought up all kinds of silly jokes, with the help of some of the actors they became even cruder, and it seemed as if the whole of the old building were being haunted by the Wild Hunts, nor did the nuisance end until it was time to dine.

The Count had conducted Melina into a large room which was still part of the old house, but was connected to the new one by a gallery; here a small theatre could be very well set up. In this room the perceptive master of the house indicated how he would like everything to be arranged.

The work was now undertaken in great haste, the stage structure was put up and decorated, and whatever decorations could be found and utilized amidst the luggage brought with them they used, constructing the rest with the help of some skilled men of the Count's household. Wilhelm lent a hand himself, helping to define the perspective and to measure the outlines, and being much concerned that there should be nothing inappropriate about the theatre. The Count, who often came by, was very pleased with the work, showed them how they ought to be doing what they were in fact doing, and in the process showed unusual knowledge of every art.

Now the rehearsing really started in earnest, and they would have had space and time enough for this, if they had not been continually disturbed by the many strangers present. For new guests arrived daily, and each one wished to inspect the theatre company.

Chapter Five

The Baron had kept Wilhelm in suspense for some days in the hope that he was still to be specially presented to the Countess.

'I have told this excellent lady so much about your clever and sensitive plays that she can't wait to speak to you and to have one or two of them read aloud to her. Keep yourself in readiness to come over at the first sign, for you are certain to be summoned the next time there is a quiet morning.' He then indicated to him the epilogue that he should read first and with which he would commend himself quite particularly. The lady regretted very much, the Baron continued, that he had arrived at such a disturbed time and that he was having to make do in a poor way in the old house with the rest of the theatre company.

After this Wilhelm selected with great care the play with which he should make his début in fashionable society. 'Up to now,' he said, 'I have worked quietly for myself, being applauded only by individual friends; for a time I despaired of my talent completely, and I must still be anxious as to whether I am on the right path, and whether I possess as much talent for the theatre as I do inclination. The experiment is far more risky than elsewhere, in the presence of such practical connoisseurs in a private room where no illusion can take place, and yet I would not like to be backward, but would be glad to associate this pleasant experience with my earlier joys and to extend my hopes of the future.'

He then went through a number of the plays, read them with the greatest care, made corrections here and there, recited them out loud in order to be truly skilful in speech and expression, and put into his pocket that play which he had rehearsed the most and which he believed would do him most credit, when one morning he was requested to appear before the Countess.

The Baron had assured him that she would be on her own with a close friend. When he entered the room, the Baroness von C—— came towards him with much friendliness, expressed pleasure in making his acquaintance, and presented him to the Countess, who was just having her hair attended to and who received him with amicable words and looks, though near her chair he unfortunately saw Philine kneeling and doing all sorts of silly things. 'The beautiful child has been singing various songs for us,' the Baroness said. 'But do finish off the little song you started, so that we don't miss any of it.'

Wilhelm listened to the little item with great patience, wishing that the hairdresser would leave before he began his reading. He was offered a cup of chocolate, and the Baroness herself proferred him the biscuits to go with it. None the less he did not enjoy the breakfast, for he desired too intensely to read to the beautiful Countess something that might arouse her interest and with which he might please her. Philine also was only too much in his way, for she had already frequently been irksome to him as a listener. He looked with distress at the hairdresser's hands and with every moment that passed he hoped all the more for the completion of the hair-arrangement.

Meanwhile the Count had entered and was talking about the guests that were expected today, about the programme for the day, and about any other domestic matters that might come up. When he went out, some officers requested permission to be allowed to pay their respects to the Countess, because they would have to be away before dinner. In the meantime the servant had finished, and she let the gentlemen come in.

While these things were going on, the Baroness made efforts to entertain our friend and to pay him a great deal of attention, which he received with respect, though somewhat distractedly. He felt for the manuscript in his pocket a number of times, hoped for every coming moment, and he almost lost his patience when a dealer in fancy goods was admitted who opened the cardboard containers, boxes and cases unmercifully one after the other and proferred each variety of his wares with an importunity characteristic of this species.

The company increased. The Baroness looked at Wilhelm and spoke quietly to the Countess; he noticed it without understanding the reason, and this at last became clear to him at home when he took his leave after waiting an hour anxiously and in vain. He found a handsome English portfolio in his pocket. The Baroness had been able to slip it to him secretly, and immediately afterwards the Countess' little black servant-boy followed, bringing him a tastefully embroidered waistcoat, without making it really clear where it had come from.

Chapter Six

The mixed feelings of annoyance and gratitude spoiled the rest of his day until he found employment again towards evening, when Melina revealed to him that the Count had spoken of a prologue that was to be performed in honour of the Prince on the day of his arrival. The Count wanted the qualities of this great hero and philanthropist to be personified in the work, Melina reported. These virtues were to step on the stage together, proclaim his praises and finally encircle his bust with wreaths of flowers and laurel, while his initials together with the princely hat should gleam translucently. The Count had entrusted to him the task of looking after the versification and the other arrangements connected with this piece, and Melina hoped that Wilhelm, for whom this was something easy, would be pleased to assist him here.

'What!' Wilhelm exclaimed with annoyance, 'have we no way of honouring a prince, who in my opinion merits a very different sort of praise, other than portraits, initials and allegorical figures? How can a man of reason be flattered to see himself set up *in effigie* and his name shimmering on oiled paper! I very much fear that the allegories would give rise to many ambiguities and jokes, especially with our wardrobe being what it is. If you want to do the play or to get someone to do it, I can have nothing against it, only I do ask to be excused from this.'

Melina apologized, saying that it was only an approximate idea suggested by the Count, who in any case would leave the arranging of the play completely to them. 'I shall be really happy to make some contribution to the entertainment of these excellent ladies and gentlemen,' Wilhelm went on, 'and my Muse has up to now not had so pleasant a duty as to make herself heard, even if only stammeringly, in the praise of a prince who deserves so much respect. I will think about the matter; perhaps I shall succeed in presenting our little troupe in such a way that we can at least achieve some effect.'

From this moment on Wilhelm thought keenly about the task. He had already sorted everything out into some order before he went to sleep, and early next morning the plan was ready, the scenes sketched out, and indeed some of the more important sections and songs had already been versified and put down on paper.

In the morning Wilhelm at once hastened to have a word with the Baron and presented him with his plan. The Baron was very pleased, but he did show some surprise. For the previous evening he had heard the Count talking about a quite different play which according to his statement was to be versified.

'It doesn't seem likely to me,' Wilhelm rejoined, 'that it was the Count's intention to have just that play worked out, as he had outlined it to Melina; unless I am mistaken, he merely wanted to give us a hint to put us on the right track. The person who is an amateur and connoisseur shows the artist what he wants, and then leaves to him the worry of producing the completed work.'

'Not at all,' the Baron replied; 'his Highness the Count is relying on the play being presented according to his specifications, and in no other way. Your play has a remote resemblance to his idea, it is true, and if we want to carry it through and to deflect him away from his first thoughts, we shall have to effect it by calling on the ladies. The Baroness is especially knowledgeable about arranging such operations in a masterly fashion; the question is whether the plan will please her so much that she will be willing to take up the scheme, and then it is sure to work out.'

'We need the ladies' help in any case,' Wilhelm said, 'for our personnel and wardrobe are not adequate for carrying out the scheme. I've had my eye on some pretty children who run about the house and who belong to the valet and the steward.'

He then besought the Baron to acquaint the ladies with his plan. The Baron soon came back and brought the news that they would like to speak to him themselves. This very evening, when the gentlemen sat down to their game, which in any case would become more serious than usual because of the arrival of a certain general, they would withdraw to their rooms under the pretext of an indisposition, he would be brought in by means of a secret stairway and could then state his case as well as possible. This kind of secret would now give the affair a double attraction, and the Baroness in particular would be as pleased as a child in looking forward to this rendezvous and would be all the more pleased because it would be arranged secretly and cleverly against the Count's will.

Towards evening at the time arranged, Wilhelm was fetched and cautiously led upstairs. The way in which the Baroness came towards him in a little private room reminded him for a moment of previous happy times. She led him into the Countess' room, and now followed many questions and investigations. He presented his plan with the maximum of warmth and vivacity, so that the ladies were completely attracted to it, and our readers will allow us to acquaint them briefly with it as well.

In a rustic setting children were to introduce the play with a dance which depicted that game where one person has to go round and gain a place from the other. After that they were to alternate with other pleasantries and end up by singing a cheerful song to a constantly returning round dance. Then the Harpist was to come on with Mignon, arouse curiosity and attract the interest of several country people; the old man was to sing various songs in praise of peace, quiet and happiness, and then Mignon was to dance the egg dance.

They are disturbed in this innocent happiness by martial music, and the company is set upon by a troop of soldiers. The male characters take up the defence and are overcome, the girls flee and are fetched back. Everything seems to be collapsing in the turmoil when a personage about whose role the poet was still uncertain comes along and restores quiet with the news that the army-leader is not far off. At this point the hero's character is delineated with the finest traits, security is promised in the midst of the weapons, and a curb is put on presumption and violence. A general festivity takes place in honour of the magnanimous army-leader.

The ladies were very content with the plan, only they maintained there must of necessity be something allegorical in the play in order to make it pleasing to his Highness the Count. The Baron made the suggestion that the soldiers' leader should be denoted as the presiding genius of dissonance and violence; but that Minerva would have to come finally to put him in chains, to give news of the hero's arrival and to sing his praise. The Baroness undertook the task of convincing the Count that the plan which he had suggested, only with some changes, had been carried out; in doing this, she expressly insisted that at the end of the play the bust, the initials and the princely hat would have to appear at all costs, because otherwise all the negotiating would be in vain.

Wilhelm, who had already imagined in his mind's eye how subtly he would praise his hero through the voice of Minerva, only gave way on this point after long resistance; however, he felt that he had been constrained in a very pleasant manner. The Countess' beautiful eyes and her attractive manners would indeed have easily persuaded him to renounce even the most beautiful and agreeable invention, even the so intensely desired unity of a structure and all appropriate details and to act against his poetic conscience. Likewise his middle-class conscience had to face a hard fight, as the ladies insisted expressly, when the roles were being more definitely apportioned, that he should act too.

Laertes had been allocated the part of that violent war-god, and Wilhelm was to act the country people's leader, who had some very charming and emotional lines to speak. After he had resisted for a time, he had to give way finally; in particular he could find no excuse as the Baroness put it to him that the stage here in the house was to be regarded in any case only as an amateur theatre, where she would be glad to act as well, if only a suitable introduction could be made. At this the ladies let our friend go with much friendliness. The Baroness assured him that he was an incomparable person and accompanied him as far as the little stairway, where she bade him goodnight with a pressure of the hand.

Chapter Seven

Fired with enthusiasm by the genuine interest which the ladies were taking in the matter, he found that the plan, which had come yet closer to his mind through being narrated, had turned into something quite full of life. He spent the greater part of the night and the next morning in the most careful versification of the dialogue and the songs.

He was pretty well ready when he was summoned into the new house, where he heard that their Highnesses, who were just having breakfast, wanted to speak to him. He stepped into the assembly room; the Baroness was again the first person to come up to him, and using the pretext of wishing good morning to him, she whispered to him in secret: 'Don't say anything about your play except what you are asked.'

'I hear that you are quite busy,' the Count called to him, 'and are working on my prologue which I wish to present in honour of the Prince. I consent to your introducing a Minerva into the play, and I will think out in good time how the goddess is to be dressed so that no exception can be taken to the costume. This is why I am having all the books which contain a picture of her fetched from the library.'

At that very moment some servants entered the room carrying big baskets full of books of all sizes.

Montfaucon[1], the collections of classical statues, cameos and coins, and all kinds of mythological writings were consulted and the figures compared. But even this was not enough! The Count's excellent memory recalled for him all the Minervas that might still be found on frontispieces, vignettes and the like. Therefore one book after another had to be procured from the library, so that finally the Count was sitting in a heap of books. In the end, unable to think of any more Minervas, he called out with a laugh: 'I'll bet there isn't a single Minerva left in the library now, and it might well be the first time that a collection of books has had to be so completely deprived of the picture of their tutelary goddess.'

The whole group expressed pleasure at the idea, and in particular Jarno, who had urged the Count on to have ever more books fetched along, laughed quite immoderately.

'Well now,' said the Count, turning to Wilhelm, 'is it of prime

1. Bernard de Montfaucon (1655-1741), French scholar and critic, author of *L'antiquité expliquée et représentée en figures,* 1719-24. (Tr.)

importance, which goddess you have in mind? Minerva or Pallas? The goddess of war or of the arts?'

'Would it not be most appropriate, your Excellency,' Wilhelm replied, 'if we didn't express ourselves definitely in this respect, and for the very reason that she does play a double role in mythology, if we were to cause her to appear here in her dual function. She heralds a warrior, but only in order to pacify the people, she praises a hero by extolling his humane qualities, she overcomes violence, and restores happiness and peace among the people.'

The Baroness, becoming anxious that Wilhelm might give himself away, quickly interposed with the Countess' tailor, who had to give his opinion as to how such a classical costume could be best produced. This man, who was experienced in fancy-dress work, was able to make the task a very easy one, and as Madame Melina, in spite of her advanced pregnancy, had taken the part of the heavenly maiden, he was told to take her measurements, and the Countess indicated, though with some resentment on the part of her maids, the clothes from the wardrobe which were to be cut up for this purpose.

Once more the Baroness managed to take Wilhelm skilfully to one side and soon afterwards she let him know that she had seen to the other things. She immediately sent to him the musician who conducted the Count's private orchestra, so that he could either compose the necessary pieces or else search out suitable tunes from the supply of music. Now everything went as they wished it, the Count had no further questions about the play, but was chiefly concerned with the translucent scenic decoration which was to surprise the audience at the end of the play. His inventiveness and the cleverness of his confectioner[1] brought about a really pleasant form of illumination. For in the course of his travels he had seen the greatest festivities of this kind, he had brought back with him many engravings and drawings, and he knew how to indicate very tastefully what was needed.

Meanwhile Wilhelm had finished his play, gave everyone his part, took over his own role, and the musician, who was at the same time very knowledgeable about dancing, arranged the ballet, and so everything made the best of progress.

There was only one unexpected obstacle that threatened to cause an awkward gap for him. He had promised himself the

1. An eighteenth-century confectioner could be responsible not only for producing sweet confectionery, but also for providing decorations for festive occasions. (Tr.)

greatest effect from Mignon's egg dance; how surprised he was therefore when the child in her usual dry manner refused to dance for him, protesting that she was his now and would be going on the stage no more. He tried to persuade her with all kinds of exhortation and did not desist until she began weeping bitterly, falling at his feet and crying out: 'Dear Father! Do keep away from the stage yourself too!' He did not heed this hint, and went on thinking how he might make the scene interesting by giving it another turn.

Philine, who took the part of one of the country girls and was to sing solo in the round dance and to teach the lines to the chorus, was looking forward to this exuberantly. In general, things were going completely according to her wishes; she had her own room, was always about the Countess, whom she entertained with her silly tricks and for these received some present every day; a dress was being tailored especially for her too for this play; and as she had an easy, imitative nature, she had soon picked up in the company of the ladies as much as was appropriate for herself, and within a short time she was full of good breeding and good manners. The attentions of the master of horse increased rather than lessened, and since the officers also brought their pressures to bear on her and she found herself in an environment offering such ample provisions, she thought that she too would play the part of someone demure and coy and in a neat way give herself practice in the assumption of a certain elegant manner. Cool and artful as she was, within a week she was familiar with the weaknesses of the whole household so that, had she been able to act with deliberate purpose, she could have made her fortune quite easily. But here too she only made use of her advantage in order to amuse and enjoy herself, and to be impertinent where she observed that this could happen without risk.

The parts had been learnt, a dress-rehearsal of the play was ordered, the Count intended to be there, and his lady began to be worried about how he would receive it. The Baroness summoned Wilhelm secretly, and the closer the time drew near, the more embarrassment became evident; for indeed there was just nothing at all of the Count's idea left. Jarno, who happened to come in then, was let into the secret. This pleased him very much, and he was ready to offer the ladies his good offices. 'It would certainly be a bad thing, my lady,' he said, 'if you were not to find your way out of this business on your own; but I will hold myself in reserve in case of need.' The Baroness then told how she had up to now recounted the whole play to the Count, but only in parts and without putting it in order, so that he was prepared for everything in single episodes; but it was true, she said, that he believed that the whole would coincide with his own conception. 'This evening I'll sit by him in the rehearsal and try to distract him. I've already instructed the confectioner to make the final scenic effect very impressive, but at the same time to let there be some small fault.'

'I know of a court where we could make use of such active and sensible friends as you are,' Jarno added. 'If you can't make progress this evening with your arts, give me a sign, and I will call the Count outside and not let him in again until Minerva appears and assistance is to be expected from the illumination effect. For some days I have had something to reveal to him concerning his brother which I have gone on postponing telling him for various reasons. This will also be a distraction for him, and it is true, not the pleasantest.'

Some business prevented the Count from being present at the beginning of the rehearsal, and then the Baroness kept him occupied. Jarno's help was not at all necessary. For as the Count found enough to correct, improve and put in order, he became completely taken up with these things, and since Madame Melina spoke at the end of the play as he wanted her to and the illuminations went off well, he showed himself as being fully satisfied. It was not until it was all over and people were turning to gaming that the differences seemed to strike him, and he began to consider whether after all the play really was his invention. At the given signal Jarno came in from the reserve position, the evening took its course, the news that the Prince was really coming was confirmed, several sallies forth on horseback were made to see the advance guard encamped in the neighbourhood, the house was full of noise and disturbance, and our players, who were not always looked after in the best possible manner by the reluctant servants, had to spend their time in expectations and preparations in the old building, without anybody remembering them in particular.

Chapter Eight

At last the Prince came; the general officers, the staff officers and the rest of the retinue that arrived at the same time, the many people who came along, either as visitors or for business purposes, made the palace like a beehive when the bees are about to swarm. Everyone pressed round to see the excellent Prince, everyone admired his geniality and condescension, everyone was surprised to perceive in the hero and army-leader the most affable courtier.

All members of the household were ordered by the Count to be at their posts for the arrival of the Prince; no actor was to let himself be seen, because the intention was that the festivities that had been prepared should take the Prince by surprise. And so in the evening too, when he was conducted into the large, well-lit assembly room, which was decorated with woven tapestries from the previous century, he did not seem to be at all prepared for a play, much less for a prologue in his own honour. Everything went off very well, and after the performance the troupe had to come along and present itself to the Prince, who was able to ask some questions of everybody in the most friendly fashion and to say something to everyone in the most agreeable manner. Wilhelm as the author had to step forward separately, and he likewise was praised for his part.

Nobody made any special enquiries about the prologue, and in a few days it was as if nothing of the sort had been performed, except that Jarno occasionally spoke about it with Wilhelm and praised it in a discerning manner; only he added: 'It's a pity that you play for empty nuts with empty nuts.' The phrase remained in Wilhelm's mind for several days; he did not know how he should interpret it nor what he was supposed to get from it.

Meanwhile the company performed every evening to the best of their abilities, and did all that was possible to attract the attention of the audience. Unmerited applause cheered them, and in their old house they now really believed that the great concourse was pressing round on their account, that the crowd of strangers was being attracted by their performances and that they were the centre around which and for whose sake everything turned and moved.

Wilhelm alone noticed precisely the opposite, to his great annoyance. For although the Prince attended the first performances from start to finish with the greatest conscientiousness, esconced in his armchair, he none the less seemed gradually to excuse himself in a agreeable way from them. Precisely those people whom Wilhelm had found to be the most understanding in conversations only spent fleeting moments in the auditorium; moreover, they sat in the ante-room, played cards, or appeared to be talking about business affairs.

Wilhelm was very annoyed that for all his continuing efforts he did not receive as much applause as he would have liked. In choosing the plays, in copying the parts, in the frequent rehearsals and in any other business that might come up, he acted as eager assistant to Melina, who in the end let him do as he wished, being quietly aware of his own inadequacy. Wilhelm memorized the parts industriously and performed them with warmth, vivacity and as much propriety as the small amount of training which he had given himself allowed.

The continued interest of the Baron, however, removed all misgivings from the rest of the troupe, when he assured them that they were achieving the greatest of effects, in particular in the performance of one of his own plays; he only regretted that the Prince had an exclusive liking for French drama, whereas some of his own people, among whom Jarno was especially prominent, gave an impassioned preference to the monsters of the English stage.

If in this way now the art of our actors was not noted and admired in the best possible manner, their personalities were not completely indifferent to the audiences, both male and female. We have already indicated above that the actresses attracted the attention of young officers right from the start; but subsequently they were more fortunate and made more important conquests. However, we will keep silent about this and observe simply that Wilhelm became daily more interesting to the Countess, just as within him too a quiet inclination towards her began to develop. She could not keep her eyes off him when he was on the stage, and he soon seemed to be directing his acting and speaking only towards her. Looking at each other was an ineffable delight for them, and to this their harmless minds gave themselves up without cherishing wishes of a more adventurous kind, nor being anxious on account of any consequences.

Just as two guards talk quietly and cheerfully together across a river which separates them without thinking of the war in which their two sides are engaged, so the Countess and Wilhelm exchanged meaningful glances across the huge chasm of birth and class, and each believed that on his or her side they might safely indulge their feelings.

The Baroness meanwhile had picked out for herself Laertes who particularly pleased her as a sturdy, cheerful young man and who, although very much a misogynist, none the less did not scorn the occasional adventure and this time really would have been fascinated against his will by the kindness and engaging character of the Baroness, had not the Baron chanced to do him a good turn, or if you like, a bad one, by making him more closely acquainted with the opinions of this lady.

For when Laertes on one occasion was singing her praises loudly and giving her preference above all other members of her sex, the Baron jokingly interposed: 'I can already see the way things are; our dear friend has once more gained an inmate for her stables.' This unhappy image, which pointed only too clearly to the dangerous caresses of a Circe, annoyed Laertes beyond measure, and he could not listen without irritation to the Baron, who continued mercilessly:

'Every stranger believes that he is the first for whom such pleasant behaviour is intended; but he is making a tremendous mistake, for we have all of us at one time been led along this way; man, youth, or boy, whoever he may be, has to yield to her for a time, has to be attached to her and be desirously concerned about her.'

Nothing can be a more unpleasant surprise to the happy man, who, as he enters the gardens of an enchantress, is received by all the bliss of an artificial springtime, than the unexpected advent of some transformed predecessor who grunts at him, when his ear is hearkening for the nightingale's song.

After this discovery Laertes was thoroughly ashamed that his vanity had misled him once more into thinking some good, if only to the slightest degree, of any woman at all. He now neglected her completely, attached himself to the master of horse with whom he fenced conscientiously and went hunting, but behaved in rehearsals and performances as if this were a matter of secondary importance.

The Count and the Countess often summoned a number of members of the troupe in the mornings, and everybody constantly found reason to envy Philine's undeserved good fortune. The Count often had his favourite, the Pedant, with him for hours on end at his dressing-table. This man was provided with clothes gradually and equipped and fitted out with everything except watch and snuff-box.

On a number of occasions also the whole troupe was requested to come before the persons of high rank. They considered this to be the highest honour and did not notice that at the very same time huntsmen and servants were bringing in a number of dogs and were parading horses in the palace courtyard.

Wilhelm had been told that he should find occasion to praise the Prince's favourite, Racine, and thereby to cause a good opinion of himself to be gained by the Prince. It was on one such afternoon that he found the opportunity for this, as he too had been summoned and the Prince asked whether he was also busy reading the great French dramatists; Wilhelm answered this question with a very lively 'Yes'. He did not notice that the Prince, without waiting for his reply, was already on the point of turning away to someone else, he rather insisted on holding his attention immediately and almost stood in his way as he continued, saying that he held French drama in very high esteem and read the works of the great masters with delight; that in particular it had given him sincere pleasure to hear the Prince was prepared to accord full justice to the gifts of a Racine. 'I can imagine,' he went on, 'how distinguished and exalted personages must value a poet who describes the circumstances of their more elevated situation so excellently and accurately. If I may say so, Corneille has delineated great human beings, and Racine elevated personages. When I read his plays, I can always think of the poet who lives at a brilliant court, has a great king before his eyes, associates with the best people and penetrates into human secrets as they hide behind expensively woven tapestries. When I study his *Britannicus* or *Bérénice,* I really feel as if I am at court, as if I have been initiated into great and small aspects of these dwelling-places of the earthly gods, and through the eyes of a sensitive Frenchman I see kings whom a whole nation adores, and courtiers who are envied by many thousands, in their natural shapes with all their faults and sorrows. The anecdote that Racine died of a broken heart because Louis the Fourteenth no longer looked at him and made him aware of his displeasure is for me a key to all his works, and it is impossible that a poet of such great gifts, whose life and death depend upon the eyes of a king, should not also write plays which are worthy of the applause of a king and a prince.'

Jarno had stepped up and listened to our friend with amazement; the Prince, who had not answered and had shown his approval only by a kindly glance, turned aside, although Wilhelm, who still did not realize that it was not becoming to continue a conversation in such circumstances and to wish to exhaust a topic in discussion, would gladly have gone on talking and shown the Prince that it was not without profit and imaginative feeling that he had read his favourite poet.

'Haven't you ever seen a play by Shakespeare?' said Jarno, taking him to one side.

'No,' replied Wilhelm; 'for since the time when these plays have become better known in Germany, I have not been in touch with the stage, and I don't know whether I should be pleased that an old hobby and preoccupation from former times has been renewed by chance at present. All the same, all that I have heard about those plays has made me curious to get to know at closer quarters such strange monsters which seem to stride out beyond all probability and propriety.'

'Then I will advise you to make an experiment; it can't do any harm for us to see with our own eyes even something that is strange. I will lend you a few volumes, and you can't put your time to better use than by cutting yourself off from everything and by looking, in the solitude of your old house quarters, into the magic lantern of this unknown world. It's a sin that you should waste your time in adorning these apes in a more human style and in teaching these dogs to dance. I only make one stipulation, that you don't take exception to the form; I can leave the rest to your own true feeling.'

The horses were at the door, and Jarno mounted with some other riders, in order to enjoy the hunt. Wilhelm looked after him sadly. There was still much that he would have liked to discuss with this man who, even in an unfriendly manner, did give him new ideas, ideas which he needed.

A man who is approaching a certain style of development in his energies, capabilities and ideas occasionally finds himself in a state of embarrassment out of which a good friend could easily help him. He resembles a traveller who falls into water when he is not far from the inn; if someone were to lend a hand and pull him on to the land, he would not have lost anything, apart from once getting wet, whereas if he has to get out on his own, he may find himself on the distant bank and have to make a wearisome and extended détour in order to reach his set objective.

Wilhelm began to sense that things happened differently in the world than he had thought. He saw at close quarters the important and momentous life led by the elegant and the great, and marvelled at the way they could give this life a style of easy good breeding. An army on the march, a princely hero leading it, so many warriors taking part and so many thronging admirers exalted his imagination. It was in this mood that he received the promised books,[1] and within a short time, as can be surmised, the broad current of that great genius seized hold of him and carried him to a boundless sea in which he very soon forgot and lost himself completely.

1. These are works of Shakespeare. At the beginning of Book V, chapter 5, we learn that the Shakespeare version is that of C. M. Wieland, which appeared from 1762-66 and contained 22 plays. It was through this translation that Goethe was introduced to Shakespeare. (Tr.)

Chapter Nine

The relationship of the Baron to the actors had undergone various changes in the course of their stay in the house. At first it led to satisfaction on both sides; for as the Baron for the first time in his life saw one of his plays, with which he had already enlivened an amateur theatre, in the hands of real actors and on the way to respectable performance, he was in the best of humour, proved himself to be generous, and bought from every dealer in fancy goods (of whom many appeared) little presents for the actresses, and knew how to procure extra bottles of champagne for the actors now and again; on the other hand, they for their part took a great deal of trouble with his play, and Wilhelm spared no pains in memorizing most exactly the magnificent speeches of the fine hero, whose role had been allotted to him.

In the meantime, however, some dissensions had gradually slipped in. The Baron's preference for certain actors became more noticeable from day to day, and inevitably this could not but annoy the others. He singled out his favourites in quite an exclusive way and thereby brought jealousy and disunity among the company. Melina, who in any case had no idea what to do in disputes, found himself in a very unpleasant position. Those who were praised accepted the acclaim without being particularly grateful, and those who were slighted made their annoyance felt in all kinds of ways, and could make their patron, whom until recently thay had revered, feel in one way or another that his presence among them was unwelcome; indeed there was not a little nourishment to their malicious pleasure when a certain poem, whose author was not known, caused much stir in the house. Up to now the Baron's associating with the actors had always aroused critical comment, but in a fairly refined manner; all sorts of stories had been told about him, certain incidents had been decked out and given an amusing and interesting form. Finally people started saying that a kind of craftsman's professional envy was coming into existence between himself and some of the actors who also fancied themselves as writers, and it was on this legend that the poem about which we were talking was based and which ran as follows:

Sir Baron, I'm a wretched devil,
I envy you because of your rank,
Because of your place at such high level,
Your many lovely stretches of land,

Your father's solid country seat,
His hunting and his shooting beat.

Sir Baron, you envy me, I find,
Because, poor devil that I am,
I've found Dame Nature fond and kind,
She's always been a good mother to me.
With good heart and nimble head, alas,
I was poor, but not a silly ass.

Now I would think, Sir Baron fair,
That we should leave things as they are:
You stay your father's son and heir,
And I'll remain my mother's child.
Let's live our lives without envious fights,
Not craving for each other's place,
You give up hope of poetic heights,
And I'll dispense with lordly grace.

Opinions about this poem, which was to be found in various hands in several almost illegible copies, were very divided, but nobody could surmise the author's identity, and when some people started being somewhat maliciously amused about this, Wilhelm expressed his strong opposition.

'We Germans,' he cried out, 'would deserve that our arts should remain in the contempt in which they have languished for so long, since we are unable to value men of rank who in any way wish to take an interest in our literature. Birth, rank and fortune are by no means incompatible with genius and good taste, as other nations, which count a great number of noblemen among their best brains, have taught us. If hitherto it was a miracle in Germany when a man of high birth devoted himself to science, if hitherto only a few famous names became even more famous through their interest in the arts and science, if on the other hand many came forth from the darkness and appeared like unknown stars on the horizon, this will not always be the case, and unless I am mistaken, the nation's highest class is on the way to making use of its advantages in future also in order to win the Muses' most beautiful triumphal wreath. Nothing is therefore more unpleasant for me than to see not only a man from the middle classes mocking a nobleman who knows how to value the Muses, but also people of rank themselves frightening off their own sort of people in ill-considered caprice and with a malicious pleasure that should never be condoned from a path upon which honour and contentment await everyone.'

The last statement seemed to be directed against the Count, about whom Wilhelm had heard that he found the poem really good. It is true that this gentleman, who in his own style was always used to making fun of the Baron, found such a pretext for tormenting his relative in all sorts of ways very welcome. Everyone was making his own speculations as to who could be the author of the poem, and the Count, who did not like to see himself surpassed in acumen by anybody, had an idea which he was at once ready to invoke: the poem could only have been written by his Pedant, who was a very fine fellow and in whom he had long ago noticed some element of poetic genius. In order to entertain himself thoroughly with the affair, he summoned this actor to him one morning, and the latter had to read the poem aloud in his own style in the presence of the Countess, the Baroness and Jarno; for this he received praise, applause and a present, while he could sensibly answer in the negative when the Count asked him whether he still possessed any poems from earlier times. In this way the Pedant came to be known as a poet and witty fellow, and in the eyes of those who supported the Baron, as a lampooner and base person. From this time on the Count applauded him all the more, however he acted his part, with the result that the poor man finally became puffed up with conceit, indeed almost crazy, and was wondering whether, like Philine, he could take a room in the new house.

If this plan could have been carried out at once, he might have avoided a great mishap. For while late one evening he was going to the old building and groping in the dark on the narrow path, he was suddenly attacked and held by some persons, while others soundly belaboured him and thrashed him so severely in the dark that he almost lay unconscious and only clambered up with effort to his comrades who, however much they might pretend to be indignant, took a secret pleasure at this misadventure and could scarcely conceal their laughter when they saw that he had been so thoroughly pummelled and that his new brown coat was dusty and stained, with white all over it, as if he had been having a row with some millers.

The Count, who at once received news of this, gave vent to indescribable anger. He treated this deed as if it were the greatest crime, denoted it as a breach of the peace on the property, and made his magistrate undertake the sternest inquiry. The coat with its white marks was to be a major piece of evidence. Anything in the house that could have at all to do with powder and flour was brought into the investigation, but in vain.

The Baron swore solemnly on his honour that certainly he had not at all liked that kind of joke and the Count's behaviour had not been the most friendly; but he had been able to disregard it, and he had not taken the least part in the mishap that had befallen the poet or lampooner, or whatever he might be called.

The other commotions among the visitors and the disquiet in the house soon caused the whole matter to be forgotten, and the unlucky favourite had to pay dearly for the pleasure of having worn strange feathers for a short time.

Our troupe, which performed regularly every evening and on the whole was very well treated, now began to make greater demands, the better things went with them. Within a short time they became dissatisfied with food, drink, service and accommodation, and requested their patron the Baron to look after them better and to help them to the attainment of the pleasures and comforts that he had promised them. Their complaints became louder, and the efforts of their friend to give them satisfaction became even more fruitless.

Wilhelm meanwhile hardly showed himself any more, except in rehearsals and times of performance. Locked away in one of the furthest rear rooms, where only Mignon and the Harpist were gladly admitted, he lived and had his being in the world of Shakespeare, with the result that he knew and felt nothing apart from himself.

Tales are told of magicians who with magic spells conjure up in their rooms a vast quantity of all kinds of supernatural figures. The invocations are so powerful that the room space is soon filled up, and the spirits multiply, pressing up close to the small circle that has been drawn, and moving around the circle and above the master's head in constantly turning transformation. Every corner is stuffed full and every ledge occupied. Eggs distend and gigantic forms shrivel into mushrooms. Unfortunately the necromancer has forgotten the word with which he could turn this tide of spirits and bring it again to the ebb.—Thus Wilhelm was seated, and a thousand feelings and potentialities, of which he had had no notion or idea, stirred within him with unknown movement. Nothing could snatch him out of this state, and he was very dissatisfied when anybody took the opportunity of conversing with him about what was going on outside.

Consequently he hardly paid attention when he was brought the news that a sentence was to be carried out in the courtyard of the house and a boy was to be flogged who was suspected of breaking in at night and who, since he was wearing a wigmaker's coat, might well have been one of the attackers. Admittedly the boy denied this most obstinately, and it was, therefore, not possible to punish him formally, but there was the wish to give him as a vagrant something to remember and to send him on his way, for he had been straying about in the area for some days and spending his nights in the mills, and had finally propped a ladder against a garden-wall and climbed over.

Wilhelm did not find anything particularly noteworthy about the whole business until Mignon rushed in and assured him that the captive was Friedrich, who had disappeared from the company and from our view after the quarrel with the master of horse.

Being interested in the boy, Wilhelm started up in haste and found that preparations were already being made in the court-yard. For the Count loved formality even in these sorts of cases. The boy was brought along. Wilhelm intervened and asked for the proceedings to stop, as he knew the boy and had various things to bring up on his account beforehand. He had difficulty in prevailing with his protests, and finally received permission to talk on his own with the delinquent. The latter asserted that he knew nothing at all of the affray in the course of which an actor was said to have been mishandled. All he had done was to rove round outside the house and to slip in at night with the aim of looking up Philine whose bedroom he had spied out and which he could certainly have reached too, if he had not been caught while on the way.

Wilhelm, who for the sake of the troupe's reputation was not keen on revealing the relationship, hastened to the master of horse and requested him, with his knowledge of the persons involved and of the house, to mediate in this affair and to liberate the boy.

With Wilhelm's support this droll man thought out a little story, to the effect that the boy had belonged to the troupe and had run away, but now wished again to turn up there and to be accepted by it. On that account he had the intention, it was said, of visiting some of his patrons after dark and of paying his respects to them. Futhermore, testimony was given that he had behaved well in other particulars; the ladies intervened, and he was released.

Wilhelm took him in, and he was now the third member of the strange family that Wilhelm had for some time regarded as his own. The old man and Mignon received the returning wanderer in a friendly way, and all three united to serve attentively their friend and protector and to render some kindness to him.

Chapter Ten

Every day now Philine was able to ingratiate herself more with the ladies. When they were together on their own, she mostly steered the conversation on to the subject of the men who came and went, and Wilhelm was not the last man with whom they were concerned. The clever girl perceived that he had made a deep impression on the Countess' heart; she therefore said what she knew about him, and what she did not; but took care not to bring up anything that could be construed to his disadvantage, and on the contrary acclaimed his magnanimity, his generosity and in particular his modesty in his behaviour towards the female sex. She was discreet in answering all other questions that were put to her, and when the Baroness noticed the growing fondness of her beautiful friend, she too found this discovery very welcome. For her relationships with several men, especially in the very recent past to Jarno, did not remain concealed from the Countess whose pure spirit could not notice such frivolity without disapproval and gentle reproof.

In this way the Baroness as well as Philine both had a particular interest in bringing our friend in closer contact with the Countess, and Philine was also hoping to make some progress on her own account, if the opportunity offered, and regain for herself, if possible, the lost favour of the young man.

One day when the Count had gone hunting with the rest of the company and the gentlemen were not expected back until the next morning, the Baroness came up with a prank which was completely characteristic of her; for she loved disguises, and in order to surprise the company, she appeared now as a peasant-girl, now as a page, and now as a huntsman's lad. In this way she acquired for herself the reputation of being a little fairy who is present everywhere, in particular in those places where she is least expected. She was never so pleased as when she had been acting as waitress to the company without being recognized or had been moving about among them in some other capacity, and had finally been able to reveal herself in a light-hearted manner.

Towards evening she had Wilhelm summoned to her room, and as she had something else to do just then, she asked Philine to fill in the picture for him.

He came and was surprised to find the frivolous girl in the room instead of her ladyship. She met him with a certain decorous openness of manner, which she had been practising recently, and thereby obliged him likewise to polite manners.

At first she jested in a general way about the good fortune that was following him and had at present brought him here, as she indeed noticed; then she reproached him in a pleasant way for his behaviour which up to now had been tormenting her, scolded and blamed herself, confessed that in many ways she had merited his treatment of her, gave a straightforward description of her position, which she referred to as the previous one, and added that she would have to be contemptuous of herself, if she were not capable of changing and of making herself worthy of his friendship.

Wilhelm was moved by this speech. He had too little knowledge of the world to realize that it is in fact the wholly frivolous people, those incapable of improvement, who often accuse themselves in the most emphatic manner, admitting and regretting their errors with great openness, although they have not within themselves the least strength to turn back from the path along which nature with her overwhelming power is carrying them. He could not therefore remain unfriendly towards the pretty sinner; he became involved in conversation with her and heard from her about the suggestion of a particular disguise with which it was hoped to take the Countess by surprise.

He had some misgivings about this, and did not hide them from Philine; but the Baroness, who entered at that moment, allowed him no time for doubts; on the contrary she drew him along in her direction by assuring him that it was just the right time.

It had become dark, and she led him into the Count's dressing room, got him to take off his coat and to slip into the Count's silk dressing-gown, then put on his head the cap with the red ribbon, led him into the private room and told him to sit in the big armchair and to take a book; she lit the Argand[1] lamp herself, and instructed him about what he had to do and what sort of part he was to play.

'The unexpected arrival of her husband and his bad mood will be announced to the Countess,' she said; 'she will come in, walk up and down the room a few times, then sit on the arm of the chair, place her arm on his shoulder and say a few words.' He was to keep up his role of husband as long and as well as he could; but when he finally had to reveal himself, he was to be really friendly and courteous.

Wilhelm sat restlessly enough now in this strange disguise; the

1. A type of oil-lamp constructed in the 1780's by Aimé Argand, of Geneva. (Tr.)

proposal had taken him by surprise, and the plan was put into effect before it had been considered. The Baroness had already gone out of the room again before he noticed what a dangerous position he had taken up. He did not deny that the beauty, youth and graciousness of the Countess had made some impression upon him; but as he was far removed by nature from all empty gallantry and as his principles did not allow him to think of more serious advances, he was really in no slight embarrassment at this moment. The fear of displeasing the Countess and that of pleasing her more than was right were present in equal dimensions within him.

Every feminine attraction that had ever acted upon him presented itself again to his imagination. Mariane appeared before him in her white house-gown and implored his remembrance. Philine's charm, her beautiful hair and her ingratiating manner had once more become affecting because of her very recent presence; but all this receded as if behind the haze of distance when he thought of the wonderful, radiant Countess, whose arm he was to feel about his neck in a few moments and to whose innocent caresses he had been invited to respond.

He certainly did not anticipate the strange way in which he should be got out of this embarrassment. For how great was his surprise, indeed his terror, when the door opened behind him and with the first covert glance into the mirror he quite distinctly saw the Count who entered with a light in his hand. His doubt about what he should do, whether he should remain seated or get up, take flight, confess, deny or beg forgiveness, lasted only a few instants. The Count, who had remained standing immobile in the doorway, stepped back and closed the door gently. At that moment the Baroness rushed in by the side-door, put out the lamp, seized Wilhelm from the chair and dragged him with her into the private room. He quickly took off the dressing-gown which at once went back to its usual place. The Baroness took Wilhelm's coat over her arm and hurried with him through some rooms, corridors and partitions into her own room where Wilhelm heard from her, after he had recovered his breath, that she had gone to the Countess in order to bring to her the fictitious news of the Count's arrival. ' "I already know", the Countess said; "What can have happened? I have just seen him ride in at the side-gate." ' The Baroness had been terrified and had at once run to the Count's room in order to take Wilhelm away.

'Unfortunately you came too late!' Wilhelm cried; 'the Count was in the room just now and saw me sitting there.'

'Did he recognize you?'

'I don't know. He saw me in the mirror, just as I saw him, and before I knew whether it was a ghost or he himself, he stepped back again and shut the door behind him.'

The Baroness' embarrassment increased when a servant came to summon her and indicated that the Count was with his lady. She went along with a heavy heart and found the Count quiet and withdrawn, but gentler and more friendly than usual in his remarks. She did not know what to think. They talked about incidents during the hunt and the reasons for his rather early return. The conversation soon dried up. The Count became quiet, and the Baroness could not help being struck when he asked about Wilhelm and expressed the wish that he should be called so that he could read something aloud.

Wilhelm, who had put his own clothes on again and to some extent recovered in the Baroness' room, responded to the command with some apprehension. The Count gave him a book from which he read out an adventurous tale, not without anxiety. His tone of voice had an uncertain, tremulous quality which fortunately was appropriate to the contents of the story. The Count made friendly gestures of approval a number of times and commended the particular expressiveness of the reading when he finally released our friend.

Chapter Eleven

Wilhelm had scarcely read some plays by Shakespeare when their effect on him was so great that he was not able to continue further. His whole spirit came into a turmoil. He sought an opportunity to talk to Jarno and could not thank him enough for the happiness procured him.

'I indeed foresaw,' said Jarno, 'that you would not remain unreceptive to the excellences of the most extraordinary and amazing of all writers.'

'Yes, indeed,' Wilhelm cried, 'I don't remember that a book, a person or any happening in life produced such great effects upon me as the wonderful plays which I have got to know as a result of your kindness. They seem to be the work of a heavenly spirit who comes close to people in order to introduce himself to them in the gentlest way possible. They are not literary works! You believe that you are standing before the huge, open books of fate in which the high wind of life at its most agitated storms, turning the pages back and forth rapidly and with violence. I am so astonished and disconcerted by the strength and delicacy, the violence and calm, that I can only wait with longing for the time when I shall be in a position to be able to go on reading.'

'Bravo!' said Jarno, offering our friend his hand and shaking hands with him, 'that's how I wanted it! And the consequences that I hope for will certainly also not be missing.'

'I wish that I could reveal to you everything that is going on inside me at present,' replied Wilhelm. 'In Shakespeare's plays I find the fulfilment and development of all premonitory feelings that I have ever had about mankind and its destiny, and which have been with me, unnoticed by myself, from childhood onwards. It seems as if he were revealing to us all enigmas, but without our being able to say that the word of solution is to be found here or there. His characters seem to be natural human beings, and yet they are not. These most secret and most complicated creatures of nature act before us in his plays as if they were clocks whose dial and case have been made of crystal; according to their designation they indicate the course of the hours, and at the same time the wheels and spring-mechanism that drive them can be recognized. These few glances that I have cast into Shakespeare's world stimulate me more than anything else to make quicker progress in the real world, to mingle in the flood of destinies that are decreed for it, and at some future time, if I should succeed in this, to draw forth from the great sea of true nature a few cupfulls and bestow them from the stage upon the thirsting public of my native country.'

'How pleased I am about the state of mind I see you in,' Jarno rejoined, placing his hand upon the shoulder of the excited young man. 'Don't let go the intention of transferring to an active life, and hasten to make sound use of the good years that are granted to you. If I can be of help to you, this shall take place with all my heart. I still haven't asked you how you came into this company, for which you can be neither born nor educated. So much I can hope and perceive, that you have aspirations away from here. I know nothing about your origins nor your domestic circumstances; consider what you would like to confide to me. I can only tell you this much, the times of war in which we live can bring about quick changes of fortune; if you would like to dedicate your strength and talents to our service and, if need be, not be afraid of danger, I have at this moment the opportunity to put you in a position which later on you will not regret having filled for a time.' Wilhelm could not thank him enough and was readily willing to tell the whole story of his life to his friend and protector.

In the course of this conversation they had strayed a long way into the park and had come to the highway going through it. Jarno stood still a moment and said: 'Think over my proposal, make up your mind, give me your answer in a few days and trust me. I can assure you that up to now it has been bewildering to me how you could lower yourself with such people, and how, simply in order to be able to be live to a certain extent, you have had to attach your affections to a vagrant singer of ballads and to a silly hybrid creature.'

He had not finished what he wanted to say when an officer came up hurriedly on horseback, followed by a groom with a led horse. Jarno greeted him in a lively manner. The officer leapt from his horse, both embraced and talked with one another while Wilhelm, taken aback by the last words of his warlike friend, stood on one side preoccupied with his own thoughts. Jarno was leafing through some papers which the person who had just arrived had handed over to him; but the latter went up to Wilhelm, offered him his hand and called emphatically to him: 'I meet you in good company; follow the advice of your friend and in this way fulfil at the same time the wishes of a stranger who takes a cordial interest in you.' He spoke, embraced Wilhelm, and clasped him to his bosom vivaciously. At the same time Jarno came along and said to the stranger: 'It's best for me to ride in with you, then you can obtain the necessary orders, and you can ride off again before nightfall.' Both mounted the horses and left our surprised friend to his own thoughts.

Jarno's last words were still sounding in his ears. It was unbearable for him to see the two human beings who had innocently gained his affection disparaged in such an extreme way by a man whom he respected so much. The strange embrace of the officer, whom he did not know, made little impression on him; it occupied his curiosity and his imagination for a moment; but Jarno's words had touched him to the quick; he had been deeply wounded, and now on his way back he burst out with reproaches against himself that he had been willing to misunderstand and forget only for a moment Jarno's hard-hearted coldness that showed from his eyes and all his gestures. 'No!' he called out. 'You withered man of the world, you only imagine that you can be a friend! All that you may wish to offer me is not worthy of the feeling which binds me to these unhappy people. How fortunate that I have found out in time what I would have to expect from you!'

He clasped Mignon, who was just coming towards him, in his

arms and called out: 'No, nothing shall separate us, you good little creature! The apparent shrewdness of the world shall not induce me to leave you nor to forget what I owe you.'

The child, whose intense caresses he was accustomed at other times to refuse, was pleased at this unexpected expression of fondness and clung to him so tightly that it was only with difficulty that he could eventually get loose from her.

From this time onwards he paid more attention to Jarno's actions, which did not all seem praiseworthy to him; in fact, various things came about that thoroughly displeased him. Thus, for example, he had a strong suspicion that the poem about the Baron, for which the poor Pedant had had to pay so dearly, was Jarno's work. As the latter had made fun of the incident in Wilhelm's presence, our friend believed that he could recognize in this the sign of a much depraved heart; for what could be more malicious than to mock an innocent person for whose sufferings one was responsible, without contemplating either satisfaction or recompense. Wilhelm would gladly have initiated this himself, for a very strange chance had put him on the track of the perpetrators of that nocturnal misdeed.

It had always been possible to conceal from him hitherto that some young officers, in the lower assembly room of the old house, spent whole nights with some of the actors and actresses in merry-making. One morning, when he had got up early according to his custom, he chanced to come into the room and to encounter the young gentlemen who were in the act of making their toilet in a very strange way. They had been rubbing chalk into a bowl with water and were putting the paste with a brush on to their waistcoats and trousers, without taking them off, and were thus restoring the cleanliness of their wardrobe in the quickest way possible. The Pedant's coat, with its white dust-marks and stains, came to our friend's mind, as he wondered at these operations; the suspicion became all the stronger when he learned that some relatives of the Baron were in the company.

In order to come closer on the track of this suspicion, he attempted to occupy the young gentlemen with a little breakfast. They were very lively and told many merry stories. One man especially, who had been engaged in recruitment for a time, could not praise highly enough the cunning and enterprise of his captain who knew how to draw all kinds of people to him and how to dupe everyone in his own way. He recounted in detail how young people of good house and careful upbringing had been deceived by all sorts of false pretences of a decent situation, and laughed heartily at the fools who in the first place had had so much satisfaction at seeing themselves esteemed and selected by a reputable, brave, sensible and generous officer.

How Wilhelm blessed his protective spirit who showed him so unexpectedly the abyss whose edge he had approached so innocently. He now saw in Jarno nothing but a recruiting officer; the embrace of the strange officer was easily explicable to him. He detested the opinions of these men and from that moment on avoided coming together with anyone who wore a uniform, and consequently the news that the army was to move further forward would have been very pleasant to him, if he had not had to fear at the same time that he would be banished, perhaps for ever, from the proximity of his beautiful friend.

Chapter Twelve

Meanwhile the Baroness had spent several days tormented by worries and dissatisfied curiosity. For the Count's behaviour since that adventure was a complete mystery to her. He had departed completely from his usual manner; none of his accustomed jokes were heard. His demands from the company and from his servants had grown far fewer. There was little in the way of pedantry and a domineering nature to be noticed, on the contrary he was quiet and withdrawn; however, he seemed to be cheerful and really a different person. When there was reading aloud, to which occasions he occasionally gave the impetus, he chose serious, often religious books, and the Baroness lived in constant fear that behind this apparent quiet a secret resentment might be hiding, a tacit intention of avenging the outrage that he had chanced to discover. She therefore decided to take Jarno into her confidence, and she could do this all the more easily as her relationship with him was one where people usually are accustomed to withholding very little. Recently Jarno had become her close friend; but they were sensible enough to conceal their affection and their pleasures from the noisy world around them. It was only from the eyes of the Countess that this new romance had not escaped, and most probably the Baroness for her part endeavoured to occupy her friend in order to escape the quiet reproaches which she none the less had to suffer occasionally from that noble soul.

The Baroness had hardly finished telling the story to her friend when he cried out laughing: 'In that instance the old man must surely believe that he has seen himself! He is afraid that this manifestation means misfortune, perhaps even death, and now he has become tame, like all little men when they think of the process of dissolution which nobody has escaped nor will escape. But quiet! Since I hope that he still has a long time to live, let us at least take this opportunity of moulding him so that he will no longer be a burden to his wife and those living under the same roof with him.'

They now began, as soon as it was at all fitting, to talk in the Count's presence about premonitions, manifestations and the like. Jarno played the sceptic, his friend likewise, and they went so far that the Count finally took Jarno to one side, reproved him for his free-thinking and endeavoured through his own example to convince him of the possibility and reality of such stories. Jarno pretended to be surprised, dubious and finally convinced, but immediately afterwards when with his friend at dead of night he poured all the more scorn on the feeble man of the world who had now all at once been converted from his bad behaviour by a bogy and who was only still to be praised because he was awaiting an imminent misfortune, perhaps indeed death, with so much composure.

'Yet he might not be ready at all to accept the most natural consequence which this manifestation might have had', the Baronesss cried with her usual cheerfulness, which she could assume again immediately, as soon as an anxiety had been lifted from her heart. Jarno was richly rewarded, and new plans were devised to make the Count even tamer, and to stimulate and strengthen the Countess' liking for Wilhelm even more.

With this in mind the Countess was told the whole story; at first, it is true, she showed herself as angry about it, but later she became more thoughtful and in quiet moments seemed to be contemplating, pursuing and picturing that scene which had been prepared for her.

The arrangements which were now being made on all sides left no further doubt that the armies would soon move forwards and that the Prince at the same time would change his head-quarters; indeed, it was said that the Count would also leave the estate at the same time and return again to the city. Our actors therefore could easily cast their horoscopes; but Melina was the only one who took steps for himself accordingly; the others were still seeking to snatch as much pleasure as they could from the moment.

Meanwhile Wilhelm had been occupied in a particular way. The

Countess had asked him for a copy of his writings, and he saw this wish of the charming lady as the finest reward.

A young author, who has not yet seen himself in print, takes the greatest care in such a case to provide a tidy and elegant copy of his works. It is, so to speak, the golden age of authorship; one sees oneself transported into those centuries when the printing press had not as yet flooded the world with so many useless writings, when only worthwhile products of the mind were copied out and retained by the most excellent of people; and how easy it is then to draw the erroneous conclusion that a carefully prepared manuscript is also a worthy intellectual product, worth being possessed and exhibited by a connoisseur and patron.

In honour of the Prince, who was to depart shortly, another great banquet was arranged. Many ladies from the neighbourhood had been invited, and the Countess had dressed in good time. On this particular day she had put on a more sumptuous dress than she was otherwise accustomed to. Coiffure and head-dress were more choice, and she wore all her jewels. Similarly the Baroness had done all that was possible to dress herself with splendour and taste.

When Philine noticed that time was hanging heavy for the two ladies while they were expecting their guests, she suggested that Wilhelm should come, since he wished to hand over his manuscript now that it was ready and to read a few more trifles aloud. He came, and as he entered he was surprised at the figure of the Countess and at her charm, aspects which had grown only the more visible because of her adornment. He read according to the ladies' orders, only in such a preoccupied way and so badly that the listeners would have dismissed him quite soon, if they had not been so forbearing.

As often as he looked at the Countess, it seemed to him as if an electric spark appeared before his eyes; in the end he no longer knew where he should take the breath for his reading. He had always liked the beautiful lady; but now it seemed to him as if he had never seen anything more complete, and of the thousand kinds of thoughts that crossed his mind, the following might be the approximate content:

'How foolishly do so many poets and so-called men of feeling rebel against finery and splendour, and demand that women of all classes should only be seen in simple clothes that are close to nature. They rail at finery, without considering that it is not the poor adornment that displeases us when we see an ugly, or less beautiful, person dressed richly and unusually; but I would like to bring to this spot all the experts in the world and ask them if they would like to remove anything from these folds, ribbons and lace, from these puffs, curls and gleaming stones? Would they not be afraid of upsetting the pleasing impression which comes to meet them here so willingly and naturally? Yes, I may well say "naturally". If Minerva sprang forth in full armour from the head of Jupiter, the goddess seems to have stepped forward in her full adornment with gentle tread from some flower.'

He looked at her so frequently while he was reading, as if he wished to imprint this impression upon himself for ever, and read wrongly several times, without becoming confused on that account, although on other occasions he could be in despair about a mistaken word or letter, considering it a wretched stain upon a whole reading.

An intrusive noise, as if guests had driven up outside, brought the reading to an end. The Baroness went away and the Countess, on the point of closing her writing-desk, which was still standing open, took hold of a ring-box and put some more rings on her fingers. 'We shall be separated soon,' she said, fixing her eyes on the box; 'take a memento from a good friend who wishes for nothing more keenly than that things may go well with you.' She then took out a ring which displayed a shield plaited with hair and which was set with jewels. She handed it to Wilhelm who, in accepting it, was not able to say or do anything, but stood as if rooted to the ground. The Countess locked the writing-desk and sat down on her sofa.

'And I am to go away empty-handed,' Philine said, as she kneeled down at the Countess' right hand; 'just look at the fellow who has such a lot to say at the wrong time and now cannot even stammer a miserable word of thanks. Come along, sir, do your duty at least in mime, and if you yourself can't think of anything today, at least imitate me.'

Philine seized the Countess' right hand and kissed it with vivacity. Wilhelm hastily went down on his knees, took hold of her left hand and pressed it to his lips. The Countess seemed embarrassed, but without any ill will.

'Oh!,' Philine cried, 'Indeed I have already seen that much jewellery, but never as yet a lady so worthy of wearing it. What bracelets! But also what a hand! What a necklace! But also what a bosom!'

'Quiet, flatterer!' the Countess called out.

'Does that portray his lordship the Count?' Philine said, pointing to a sumptuous medallion which the Countess was wearing in rare chains on her left side.

'He has been painted as a bridegroom,' the Countess put in.

'Was he so young at that time?' asked Philine; 'You have only been married a few years, as far as I know.'

'This youthful appearance is the painter's doing,' the Countess added.

'He's a handsome man,' Philine said. 'But is it the case,' she went on, placing her hand on the Countess' heart, 'that another picture has never slipped into this hidden capsule?'

'You are very bold, Philine!' she exclaimed; I have trained you badly. Don't let me hear anything like that a second time.'

'If you are angry, I am unhappy,' Philine cried, leaping up and hurrying out at the door.

Wilhelm was still holding the most beautiful hand in his own hands. He stared unwaveringly at the bracelet which to his greatest surprise revealed the initials of his name in brilliant strokes.

'Do I really possess your hair in the costly ring?' he modestly asked.

'Yes,' she replied in a muted voice; then she pulled herself together and said, pressing his hand: 'Stand up, and say good-bye!'

'Here is my name, by the strangest chance,' he called out. He pointed to the bracelet.

'What?' cried the Countess; 'It is the cipher of a woman friend of mine!'

'These are the initials of my name. Don't forget me. Your picture is contained inextinguishably within my heart. Fare well, allow me to take flight!'

He kissed her hand and wanted to get up; but as in a dream what is most strange surprises us as it develops from what is most strange, he was holding the Countess in his arms, without knowing how it happened, her lips rested upon his, and their lively exchange of kisses bestowed on them a happiness which we can only drink from the first effervescing froth of the freshly poured goblet of love.

Her head rested on his shoulder, and no thought was given to the crumpled curls and ribbons. She had put her arm round him; he embraced her eagerly and pressed her repeatedly to his breast. Oh, that such a moment cannot last eternities, and alas for the envious fate that interrupted these short moments also for our friends!

How Wilhelm was terrified, and with what bewilderment did he start up from a happy dream, when the Countess suddenly tore herself away from him with a cry and put her hand to her heart.

He stood before her benumbed; she held her other hand in front of her eyes and called out after an interval: 'Go away, hurry!'

He still stood there.

'Leave me,' she cried, and as she took her hand away from her eyes and looked at him with an indescribable glance, she added in the loveliest voice: 'Take flight from me, if you love me.'

Wilhelm was out of the room and in his room once more, before he knew where he was.

The unhappy ones! What strange warning of chance or fate tore them apart from each other?